Returning to the Healing Oasis

Guided Meditations for Mind, Body, and Spirit

by
Sharon Moon

United Church Publishing House

Returning to the Healing Oasis
Guided Meditations for Mind, Body, and Spirit
Sharon Moon

Library and Archives Canada Cataloguing in Publication
Moon, Sharon, 1945-
Returning to the healing oasis : meditations for mind, body, and spirit/ Sharon Moon.

Includes bibliographical references.
Also available on CD, to be sold seperately or with the book.
ISBN 1-55134-147-6

1. Bible--Meditations. I. Title.

BV4832.3.M66 2006 242'.5 C2006-900321-1

United Church Publishing House
3250 Bloor St. West, Suite 300
Toronto, ON
Canada M8X 2Y4
1-800-268-3781
www.united-church.ca/ucph

Design: Carina Cruz, Graphics and Print
Cover Photos: Design Pics and Chris Dumas

Printed in Canada
5 4 3 2 1 10 09 08 07 06 050334

Contents

Preface

When I wrote my first book, *The Healing Oasis: Guided Meditations for Mind, Body, and Spirit*, I thought there might be about 200 people in the church who would be interested in this particular area of spirituality. I was overwhelmed by the response. My book is now in its third printing. This tells me that there are many of us in mainline churches who are thirsty for the deeper waters of experiencing Spirit. Talking about God is not the same as experiencing God.

I have been privileged to hear from many people about how they have been using *Healing Oasis* in their own contexts. The first response I received was from a youth leader who had used it at an event in Newfoundland, where young people found it a meaningful way to pray and to get in touch with the Spirit. Countless ministers and lay people have used it to lead groups in their churches. It was used by a chaplain in a prison with hard-case offenders and by a psychiatrist with patients. I've been told that a lot of people go to sleep with me (that is, my voice on the CD) because they have problems sleeping. Others have used it to ease their stress. I know of several people who use the CD when they are receiving chemotherapy. Several people used the meditations when they had chronic pain or were undergoing cancer treatment. Many more have found it a way to be in touch with the God who flows in and through all that is. It has been truly amazing to hear about the ways in which the Spirit has used these meditations to heal and deepen spirituality, and to promote spiritual growth.

It is because of the response to *Healing Oasis* and the request for more group meditations that I have written this second book.

My prayer is that these meditations will provide groups in churches or other spiritual settings an opportunity to dive more deeply into the living waters of the Spirit. We need communities where we can be "real" with one another about what the Spirit is doing in our lives. We need communities where we can nurture the tender shoots of spiritual growth in one another. We need communities that listen to and are responsive to the leadings of the Spirit as they make their decisions about mission and direction.

I pray that those who use these meditations and then share their experiences of the Spirit will become soul companions to one another.

Foreword

Sharon's previous work, *The Healing Oasis*, is one of the most versatile and effective resources for renewal that I have encountered in my 15 years' experience of pastoral ministry. I began to suspect this when I first tried out the audio CD at home, in the downstairs den, in the dark. Two of my three children, then ages nine and 11, came downstairs. I was ready to give up and try again later, when they sat down and began to listen to the meditation, completely silent for the next 10 to 12 minutes. If you had known my two energetic and suspicious (when it comes to church things) PK* daughters at that time, you would understand my awe. I have since used Sharon's meditations fruitfully for personal spiritual renewal, in one-on-one counselling sessions, in healing services, with seniors' home gatherings, with church committees, and as an effective central piece in congregational worship.

Sharon's deep awareness of the nature, pitfalls, and joys of the spiritual quest are evident in her writing. She brings a pastor's ear to the heart cries of spiritual seekers, faith communities, and a world deeply wounded. I relish her sensitive yet powerfully evocative language. Images and questions twine together the threads of my personal story with the scriptural story of God's presence and love in the world. This weaving has given rise to tapestries of hope, released pain, deepened insight, fostered renewal, and enduring healing.

Currently, I am working as national staff support for the development and renewal of congregations and other ministries in The United Church of Canada. I believe we stand on a threshold. A new day emerges for the church and the world. A grounded embrace of God's wise and enlivening Spirit is urgently needed. Sharon's new work, *Returning to the Healing Oasis,* could not be more timely...

For Reconnection...

This time reveals our devastating disconnection from a creation under siege. We are like those who stood on the beach talking on cell phones as the devastation of the tsunami in South Asia approached, while the animals had long since

* Preachers' kids

heard the groans of the earth and had moved to higher ground. In the "oasis" of Sharon's meditations, as I savour the succulent images of breath and storm, tree and earth, I feel my spiritual roots sinking more deeply into the rich soil of the "body of God."**

For Wholeness...

The United Church that I love has a great gift in its highly developed spiritual discipline of critique. At our best, the razor sharp edge of critical thought cuts through the delusions of regimes of oppression and injustice. When deconstruction does its work in my own psyche and soul, and I humbly offer up my brokenness to God, Sharon's meditations bathe me in the light of Spirit which imbues all creation and reminds me that I am whole, and we are all One in God.

For the Transformation of the World...

Change is everywhere and it seems to be accelerating. It can be uncomfortable, disorienting, terrifying, and it is without a doubt needed in many ways. Sharon's work becomes a resource for effective communal and global transformation because it meets people in the only place real transformation happens, deep in the heart where the Word of God is written in words seeking a singing soul.

This is a timely offering, received with deep gratitude and great hope.

Thank you, Sharon.

Rob Dalgleish,
Program Coordinator,
Congregational Renewal and Development,
The United Church of Canada

** "The Body of God" by Sallie McFague, © Augsburg Fortress, 1993.

Part I

Guidance for Those Leading Meditation

CHAPTER

1

Welcome to the Healing Oasis

The oasis is the place of living water. It is the place where you receive what you need for life. The water of the oasis creates growth in the trees and vegetation around it. These, in turn, provide shade and food for the journey. The oasis provides a welcome rest from travelling in the desert. It provides a place to stop, to nourish the body and the soul, and to renew strength and insight for the way ahead.

One comes to an oasis when one has already set out on a journey. No one would set out on a journey through the desert without knowing where the next oasis was. It is a matter of life and death. So going to an oasis is an intentional act of self-care and part of the plan for a healthy journey.

The healing oasis has become for me a profound image of small-group spirituality ministry in the church. At the oasis, you meet people who have journeyed on paths different from yours. Some have journeyed for years, while others are on their first journey. They have had different experiences en route, which they bring with them to the oasis. At the oasis, beside the waters that give life, travellers encounter one another in a very special way. They are all people on a journey. They share stories of their journey and learn from one another's experiences. They encounter one another in that "deep way" that happens when meeting fellow pilgrims.

Perhaps your path might take another direction because of what happens at the oasis. Perhaps you may leave with more wisdom for the way ahead. Perhaps you may understand your own experience in a different way because of the encounters you have shared.

However, you do not stay in an oasis. You carry on with the journey. You bring with you the gifts and insights of the encounter at the oasis, which inform the next phases of the path.

Meditation in Stress-filled Times

I feel that meditation is even more essential to wholeness and well-being now than it was seven years ago when my first book was published. During these intervening years the pace of life has sped up exponentially. As a pastor, I hear constantly about the pressure and stress of trying to find balance, of trying to create space for spiritual and family life in this economic and social climate. Constantly, we are being pulled outward to meet external demands. Partners trying to balance work with family needs and economic pressures end their day feeling heavily stressed.

Many in our congregations are under pressure to perform or face the pressures of lost employment. Many work in environments where their own values are in conflict with the values of their workplace. Others are underemployed. These are all sources of stress...and there are many more.

The cellphone and the Internet have intruded into personal space so that one is available 24 hours a day, seven days a week. People who in the past would expect a turnaround of three days, now expect an immediate response. Technology that was touted as an advancement to generate more leisure has, in fact, created far more pressure and tension.

At a certain point, it is not even the problem of external intrusion. One's own internal energy becomes addictively tuned to the hyper pace of the external world. We try to fit one more phone call, one more e-mail, one more Internet connection into an already overextended schedule. It is as if our minds are functioning at a hyper-alert frequency from which it becomes very difficult to move into relaxation. There is simply no external space or, increasingly, no internal space just "to be." Those who are more into cellphones than I do not even get the downtime of driving from one appointment to another. They are constantly "available" and continuously "on call."

Once we are "turned on" or "tuned in" to this fast pace of life, it is extremely difficult to make the shift into "being time." "Being time" is time where we are open to our own feelings, to our internal spiritual world, to the creation around us, to experiencing and encountering another person at a level that is genuine. This "being time" is essential for emotional and spiritual health. It is essential for creating the space to "be present" with another in relationship. It is essential for being aware of what we are feeling and becoming aware of the wisdom of the unconscious mind and to the workings of the Spirit. It is essential for connecting with the Holy.

Increasingly, I believe that it is essential for the health of the planet. Our political and economic decisions need to be made, not from the surface level of thinking, where power politics, emotional turmoil, and consumer values operate, but from being attuned more deeply to the health of the planet and the real world of conscious awareness and interconnected love.

Meditation is a conscious choice to create this "being time." It is a choice for mental, emotional, and spiritual well-being. It trains the mind and body to relax and centre. It moves us into depth reality and opens us to the Spirit flowing in our lives. It allows us to pay attention to what is going on in our depths, to become conscious of the emotions and patterns that control our responses. It allows us to notice where God might be inviting us to grow or change. And it invites us into a space where we treasure life, our aliveness, and the aliveness of everything around us. It invites us to cherish with compassion the gifts that are ours.

The Importance of Meditation for Families

Young families, who used to have time for such things as picnics or children's programs in our churches, now are pulled in so many directions that finding space to simply "be" is a luxury. Children, at least in my area, are so programmed that they have no space to breathe or to play between school, soccer, dance, music, hockey, swimming...and the list goes on and on.

It is not that these programs are bad. Parents who arrange these many activities for their children are trying to give them the very best opportunities that life has to offer. They are trying to situate them well in a competitive world. But these parents, who want good things for their children, are in danger of creating a generation who are even more driven than their parents, a generation who will always feel the need to look outside of themselves for entertainment.

What a spiritual void there would be if young people were to become bored with their own company, if they were to become complete strangers to the internal movements of their emotions and spirits. They would miss the experience of knowing that they are connected deeply with creation and the Sacred Source that flows through all that is.

I know one mother who has taught her hyperactive son to meditate and relax. She sits with him and they breathe together and become aware of the "now." This slows down both of them. She invites him to breathe, taking in the light of God, to remember that he is a beloved child of God, and to listen for the Spirit as he meditates. This young child is learning one of the most important lessons of life. He is being given tools to pray, to relax, to recognize that he does not have to be a prisoner of hyperactivity, to shift the energy of his feelings and thinking so that he can ground himself in being a child of God. For me, this is good parenting!

A simple way for families to begin to teach children to pray is to have a time of silence at the beginning of each meal, where the family focuses on gratitude and being thankful and asks each person to offer what they are thankful for. The responses children give sometimes surprise parents. I know a child who regularly says he is thankful "for life." Imagine if we all had that spiritual awareness!

There is not only concern for a generation of spiritually starved children, but also for parents who run themselves ragged trying to fill up their children's time with so many enriching activities. Some parents do this out of guilt that they cannot spend enough time with their kids. Some do it out of concern that their kids must have every opportunity available. Others are just trying to be the best parents possible. They have little space or time for their own spiritual health or for the health of their intimate relationships. I have great concern for the mental, spiritual, emotional, and, ultimately, physical health of people who live with this kind of stress.

I have included some very simple meditative exercises for those who want to "time shift" or to shift gears. Dr. Stephan Rechtschaffen has written an excellent book called *Time Shifting*[1], which analyzes this illness of our time, which is stress caused by constantly being "on."

Meditation for Spiritual Growth

There is another level of meditation that allows the meditator to move more deeply with some healing work or some question or issue that he or she is working on. There are meditations in this book for working with the shadow, balance, embracing transformation, and moving beyond the blame game. These offer opportunities to use meditation to deepen personal and spiritual growth.

There are some very good resources available on the power of the mind to heal the heart. One of my personal favourites is *Emotional Alchemy* by Tara Bennett-Goleman[2]. She uses meditative awareness and mindfulness to help us understand the patterns in our psyche that create problems. With compassion and understanding, we can use the awareness that comes from meditative awareness to notice our own patterns and to be empowered to make different choices for our healing.

Meditation for Physical and Spiritual Health

I use meditation as part of my ministry with those undergoing all kinds of healing journeys. In counselling, if people come in an agitated or manic state, I do not begin with talking. Instead, I will gently lead them in a meditation to ground them, relax them, and remind them to stay in their bodies. This kind of meditation reminds them that they are connected to a Loving Source that cares profoundly for them. Meditation shifts the energy and breaks the downward spiral of compulsive talking that is not healing. I can do this meditation in six or seven minutes. When the person comes out of meditation, we are then able to move more deeply in conversation about the issues they bring.

Likewise, if someone has just done a particularly painful piece of emotional work, such as recovering memories of abuse or challenging a parent or personal tyrant during counselling, I will lead her or him into a meditation that pours healing light, affirmation, and unconditional love into the person. When one does such deep work of letting go, there is an emotional space left inside. This healing spiritual energy moves in to fill up that space. It strengthens and grounds the healing work and makes it easier for the person to move forward.

I use meditation also in the Healing Pathways ministry of our congregation and for pastoral care. I have included a meditation for those going into surgery and another for those receiving treatment such as chemotherapy, dialysis, and antibiotics. There is also a bedside meditation for those sitting at the bedside of a very ill or dying person. This meditation could also be used to train pastoral care teams to be present with those who are suffering.

There are a number of meditations for individuals who are working on their personal healing journeys, such as The Tree of Life, Calm in the Storm, Formed by God, Breath of Life, and In the Palm of God's Hand.

I pray that these meditations might be a way for you to be in touch with the God in whom you live and move and have your being. These meditations are simply the container for encounters with the Holy. I know from experience that the Spirit will work in ways that I could not even begin to imagine as I write these meditations. May God bless you in your visits to the healing oasis.

CHAPTER

2

Using Guided Imagery Meditation in Groups

Background for Leaders

Overcoming Discomfort with Sharing Spiritual Experience

In the church in which I grew up, we did not talk about spiritual life. We took as literal the scripture suggesting that we were not to display our prayer life in public on street corners. Instead, as we thought scripture told us, we were to go in secret, even into a closet, to meet our God. Jesus had addressed these words to spiritually arrogant people, to those who felt that they had God in their pockets. My experience in church leads me to believe that there is a different problem in mainline congregations today. I see the problem of low self-esteem in matters of the Spirit. Too often people feel that their experiences of God are not worth sharing because they seem so ordinary and unworthy of attention.

Theology and spiritual journey have been given over to professionals. In creating a hierarchy of those "theologically trained" and those "done unto," we lose the insights of the whole community and the power to be a people of God. Any pastor who shares deeply in the life of the people can tell many stories of encountering the Spirit of God in those who felt they were not "good enough" to be part of God's family. When we do not trust or value our experience of Spirit, we do not share these experiences with others. This means that the community is not nurtured by stories of experiences of God. Using guided imagery meditation creates a space that breaks down these barriers and offers a vehicle for sharing sacred experience.

Many who have come to our meditation group have said that there is nowhere else in their lives that they are able to talk about their spiritual life. Some have tried other churches and found that talking about spiritual life was not something with which people in the community were comfortable. Some congregations only allowed a very narrow spectrum of spiritual discussion to take place. Participants said that it was an incredible relief to be able, finally, to speak about spiritual things in a safe environment. They have found a place to be in touch with God's Spirit as it moves through the scripture, in the group sharing, and in the symbolic acts that are often part of the experience.

The sharing of spiritual experience is a profound gift we give one another. It is a way for God's Spirit to become enfleshed, embodied, real. It is a way for the Spirit to indeed dwell in our midst. It gives God space to *be* the encourager, the challenger, the confronter, the hoper, the healer, the life-transformer. But it is not only God's Spirit that gets space to breathe and *be* in such a place; those who share also come to see and know themselves as vehicles of the Spirit. This is an empowering, integrating experience of being part of church community.

Introducing Imagery to the Group

If people are new to meditation, or unfamiliar with it in the Christian tradition, I would remind them that Christian meditation goes back at least as far as the desert fathers and mothers of earlier centuries. It has been practised by contemplatives throughout the generations. St. Ignatius of Loyola initiated spiritual renewal through meditations where one is invited to enter the scripture story and "live" into the images and characters. Participants also need a sense of the overall structure of a session, so that they know what to expect. This will help to create a sense of safe space. Some common concerns and questions are:

What Can I Expect?

Meditation needs practice. The first time, when one is on unfamiliar ground, meditators should be told not to set overly high expectations. Just relax and let be, and forget about achieving something.

What if I Go to Sleep?

Sometimes, when a person becomes relaxed, as at the beginning of the meditation, sleep follows. This is because the body is used to sleeping when relaxation happens. Sleep can be a real gift of God. It may be exactly what is needed on a particular occasion, but it may mean that the person is resisting either the process of the meditation, or the particular content of the meditation.

This may be a self-protection from dealing with material one is not yet ready for, or an opportunity for the depths of the soul to be reached in a more compassionate way. Each person needs to try to discern what is happening, and to decide what they want to do about it. It is possible to train the mind to stay awake during meditation, even though the body is in a state of complete relaxation. It is possible to develop an ability to be calm and to concentrate at the same time.

Am I Being Hypnotized or Controlled by the Leader?

Meditators are always free in meditation. Each person is responsible for choosing how deeply they wish to enter a meditation. They are not being hypnotized or giving over control to you as leader. They can be aware at all times of what is happening and can choose to surface from the meditation whenever they wish, and to call in any extra help, such as Christ, or a person who is a mentor, or soul companion if they feel that would be helpful. This is particularly necessary for anyone who has experienced being under another's control. Since we have all been children, we all have some experience of this. This assurance of personal power is tremendously important if a person is to trust and let go in meditation.

Should I Meditate if I Have a History of Dissociation?

Those who have dissociative disorders should consult their therapists before doing meditation. For some it is healing. Others need to be more cautious. Each person is always in control of how deeply they will enter meditation.

What if My Mind Wanders?

It is not necessary to follow slavishly the suggestions of the leader. Perhaps a person's inner soul may need to focus in one place and stay with a particular part of the meditation. It may even suggest another direction. Each person's experience is unique, and it is not helpful to try to compare, or evaluate our experience, against those of others. Learning simply to trust and honour our own experience, learning to trust the God we encounter there, is already a great value.

There are distractions and mind-wandering chatter. Some will find it almost impossible to relax and to concentrate at the beginning. Unless we are used to practising silence, the mind quickly takes over its role of trying to help. It does this by reminding us of all the things we need to remember and by putting pictures and ideas into our mind. These distract us from being able to focus and centre.

When this happens, we can give ourselves negative messages about how poor we are at meditation, how impossible it is for us to concentrate, or we can become very *earnest* about working hard to do meditation *right*.

Rather than putting a lot of energy into fighting mind-wandering mental chatter, it is better to befriend our mind. Trying too hard just creates tension that blocks effective meditation. We can thank our mind for trying to help us, but tell the mind that it can have a rest, because what we really need is to relax and practise the presence of God. It is amazing the effect that is created by this simple ritual of addressing our mind, almost as if it were a separate reality. We enlist its co-operation rather than waste energy fighting with it throughout the meditation.

Another approach is to accept the mind-wandering as a gift, as a reminder, as an indication of how much we need to meditate. Let the distraction pass gently out of awareness, rather than forcing it out by will. We might imagine these thoughts passing through our mind as clouds passing across the sky, or as leaves on a stream, gently allowing the wind or current to carry them away. Gently draw yourself back to the meditation, without moving into a self-judgmental mode.

What if I Have Difficulty Visualizing?

There are different ways of experiencing visualization. Some see things quite clearly. For others, who find this more difficult, it is better not to try to see with the eyes, but rather to allow the visualization to come to the *mind's eye*. For some it may be more like the idea of an image, or the sense or feeling of an image. It is important to refer to all the senses, and to all the ways of knowing – seeing, hearing, touching, smelling, feeling, thinking, intuiting. This honours our diversity in the ways we experience and know.

What if I Don't Remember What Happened?

Sometimes we may find we will not remember what happened in a meditation. This may mean we fell asleep, or it may mean that we were meditating very deeply and were not able to access it at that particular time. Meditations are somewhat like dreams. Some are vivid and clearly meaningful; at other times we have a dream that is vague. Sometimes the images are simply confusing. It is important to remember that the process of meditating, in and of itself, has an effect even when we are not conscious of having received any particular insights. By developing our practice of meditating, we are telling our unconscious, as well as our conscious mind, that we value internal spiritual life and that we are prepared to invest in it. This has far-reaching results of which we are often not even aware. When we value the spiritual dimension, it opens an inner door that allows the Spirit more access to our consciousness. We give permission to the unconscious and to the wisdom stored there, to release its treasure trove of gifts.

The Role of the Leader

I hope that what I share here will not only give leaders confidence for leading these specific meditations, but also will be a stepping off point for developing other guided imagery meditations in the future. Anyone who leads meditation needs to be knowledgeable and well prepared. But, once these preparations are made, one of the most important gifts of a leader is a capacity for open listening to where the Spirit is leading the group. This involves letting go of control. The leader's role is to provide a framework within which spiritual experience can happen. Leaders do not create the experience; what happens is an encounter between each meditator and the Spirit. This requires trust in the Spirit, for it requires the leader to wait upon and to expect encounter with the Spirit in meditation. No one can make it happen, however. Leaders can create an open, trusting environment and, by preparing well, can lead meditations that will be helpful. But the real work of the session happens in the hearts, minds, and souls of all those who share the experience, quite beyond the control of the person leading.

Be prepared for the unexpected. God's Spirit blows where it chooses, and we do not always know where it comes from, or where it is going.[3] In my experience of using meditation with groups, wisdom and truth have come often in the most unexpected places. Sometimes the most educated, successful participants have learned from people who have little or no status in the culture. Often the deepest experiences of God's presence come from the most vulnerable, the marginalized, the "least" in society's terms. They may have fewer barriers to hearing the good news and have more "holes through which the holy can enter." Meditation creates a group where what normally gives power in the culture is not operative. It creates a radical equality that is a foretaste of God's reign.

Leading guided imagery meditation groups requires leaders who are attentive to the needs, vulnerabilities, and strengths of group members. The leader also needs to be attentive to his or her own spiritual journey, always on the lookout for what the Spirit is doing through the group. It is important to respect the diversity and the sacredness of each person coming to the group. Meditators need to find a safe place where they can share their experience with meditation. It has to be safe to share whatever happens, whether it is a spiritual awakening or an experience that might feel negative. Unless an atmosphere of trust is created in the group, participants will not feel free to "tell it like it is." They will only share the surface facts of their journey, and everyone will be impoverished. It is important for the leader to model the kind of trust and open sharing of experience. It is most useful to assume the role of leader/participant as one who journeys alongside, rather than as one who is an expert/teacher.

When you begin a meditation group, start with a contract for a set number of weeks. I would suggest four or six weeks. This allows those who want to experiment to come to a group knowing that they will be free at the end of a set period to choose to come to another set of meditations, or to pursue other interests. We have worked with groups as large as 20, but a group under 15 is usually much better. For the sharing time following the meditation, sub-groups of six to 10 are the best.

CHAPTER

3

The Process for Meditation Groups

Before Each Session

a) The leader needs to be in touch with the scripture that is being meditated upon. She or he should have read it through several times, but also have allowed any images or feelings that emerge to resonate within.

b) It is important to think about and pray about the people who normally come to meditation.

c) Gather the materials needed for the group. I use:
- CD player and music
- cloth for a focal centre in the middle of the circle
- candle (preferably the same one each week)
- a bell to call people out of silence
- any symbols that connect with the images of the particular meditation (Suggestions are included with some of the meditations, but use your own creativity here. Sometimes a particular object seems to want to be in the centre even though you cannot understand its particular connection. I have learned to trust these intuitive suggestions.)
- additional materials to be used in the sharing (e.g. writing materials or clay)

d) Before each meditation, either at home before leaving, or before the group begins, do a silent invocation of the healing Spirit of God, invoking the presence of Christ, or of Divine Light and Wisdom on the gathering. For me, this is an essential part of the preparation. It creates an attitude of responsiveness and openness that helps the leader "let go" of her or his own agenda and the need to control the outcome of the group.

As a leader, it is important to be attentive to the need for a balance between creating the safe containing space for the group and creating the space for the "new thing God is doing in our midst." A very important way to do this is with a clear and simple process that is followed regularly, so that participants know what to expect. It is also important to agree on clearly named group norms for the ways in which the group will function together. These simple structures give a sense of security within which freedom can be experienced.

Setting Group Norms

At the first session, group norms need to be established and stated clearly. Those we have found to be important are:

a) What happens inside the group is confidential and is not to be shared outside the group.

b) When a person shares a meditation, he or she is sharing holy ground, and we need to listen to and honour that experience. Analyzing another person's meditation is almost never a good idea; it can make the person who is analyzed feel violated. As well, the interpretation usually says more about the interpreter and his or her particular issues than it does about the meditator. However, the person who is sharing the meditation may choose to ask others for insights or associations. The leader needs to keep a very close eye on this particular dynamic, and it is best named as an issue in group norms, so that the whole group can be aware when this is happening and take some responsibility for it.

c) Participants are free to share at the level they feel comfortable, and to choose *not* to share.

Session Outline

Our group has developed a very simple structure that is followed each week:

- Introduction
- Gathering
- Meditation
- Sharing
- Closure

Introduction

Each meditation has an introductory section that outlines the preparation needed for the session, the scriptures involved, and a reflection on the scriptures. You may want to share part or all of the reflection with the group, or you may find that this would be too directive. It is best not to read the scripture "cold," but rather to let the group warm up to being together first. You can also give the scripture reference(s) before the session so people have a chance to read them and think about them beforehand. This makes it easier to incorporate the scripture into your gathering activities. It is important to read the scripture aloud before the meditation, and to set it in any context that is needed.

Gathering

Gathering is a time to check in with one another. It is important to go around the circle allowing people to introduce themselves (if there are those who do not know each other), and to speak *briefly* to a specific question or thought that is suggested. Although several ideas for gathering activities are suggested in each meditation, use only one or two per session. I always allow a time of silence after the introduction of an idea or question. This allows each person to go more deeply into himself or herself for a response that might not be available on the surface, and already begins the process of moving inside. This sharing process also begins the weaving together of the community.

Each meditation has some specific suggestions that I hope you will find appropriate to the particular theme. But each group is unique, and you may have other ideas that have worked for you in other situations. You may wish to choose from some of the ideas listed below:

a) As you come to meditation, be in touch with your deepest desire, your real yearning for this time. God often meets us in this place, the place where we are most longing. Indeed we might suggest that it is through these very yearnings that we are invited into relationship, into communion with the Spirit.
   - Where is this happening for you right now?
   - Where did you sense the Spirit's presence in the past week?

b) If you had to choose a colour to represent how you feel as you come to this group, what would that be?

c) Set the theme, then read the scripture and ask participants where they find themselves in it. Is there some word, or idea, or a particular person in the scripture that connects with you at this time in your life?

d) Do a word association exercise around a text or an idea connected with the theme of the meditation.

e) Play a piece of music and invite participants to share responses. If it has words, you may ask participants to share how they feel about a particular image of God that is referred to, and to suggest others that have power and meaning for them. You may also ask for a feeling response to the music. What feelings or associations are raised for you as you listened to the music?

Meditation

There are various phases of the meditation:

- finding a comfortable position for your body-self
- preparing the spirit/body for meditation—putting the mind in a receptive, open, calm, clear state
- experiencing the imagery section of the meditation
- gradually drawing the group back to the circle and to their body-selves
- allowing silence for the experience to ground itself

Finding a Comfortable Position

At this point, suggest that participants find a position where they can be comfortable. They may need to remove shoes or glasses, loosen a belt, or lie down. It is important in meditation for the spine to be in a straight line. Whether that happens by lying, or sitting on a chair, or sitting cross-legged on the floor is irrelevant. Let participants choose whichever position is comfortable for them. Turn the lights down low, or even off if you are using an audio meditation and do not need to read it. (Check with the group if there are any members for whom darkness is a problem.) Put the CD player on if you are using music behind your own reading. There is a lot of meditative music available these days, but much of it has too much tune or melody. The more amorphous, repetitive, and non-distracting the sound, the better. It needs to be like waves on which one can rest and be supported, but beware of using water sounds as it stimulates the reflex to urinate.

If you are not using audio meditations, but are leading with your own voice, it is important to pace the meditation well. Leave long silences and pauses regularly in the meditation. If you are a beginner, practise leaving pauses that seem overly long to you, since your own perception of the passing of time is usually an underestimate of the length of silence needed for those you are guiding. Your voice needs to be gentle and flowing, coming from a deep place inside you. You need to do the body relaxation part of the meditation yourself so that your voice is coming from your centre. If you are leading meditation with a large group, use a microphone rather than projecting your voice stridently.

At the end of your sessions, ask for feedback from those you are guiding, so you will know the speed and volume that is appropriate for the group you are leading.

Preparing the Spirit/Body for Meditation

"Stilling" or "mindfulness" is the first step in meditating, before one begins the more active part of the meditation of looking for insight or depth understanding of the images. Chilean psychiatrist Claudio Naranjo distinguishes between the *mindfulness* and the *God-mindfulness* stages of meditation. At the *mindfulness* stage one is gaining awareness of the immediate sensations in one's body, the emotions one is feeling, or the thoughts that arise and pass away. At the *God-mindfulness* stage, the meditator gains wisdom and insight by focusing on an external symbol or image.[4]

It is important not to move too quickly through this stage of stilling the body because it is an essential foundation for the quality of the imaging to follow. The amount of time required for this depends upon the stress the participants bring to the time of meditation and their experience of meditation. With experience, one can learn to move into meditative state much more quickly. It is as if the brain has learned new patterns that affect the body's ability to relax and let go. For many, the paying attention to the body/spirit-self is an important source of insight, as the meditator begins to listen and pay attention to the wisdom of the body, to the wisdom of feelings, and to inner thought patterns.

Experiencing the Imagery Section of the Meditation

Since each meditation in this resource deals specifically with this aspect of the meditation, I will make some general comments here. Please note that there is repetition from meditation to meditation in the relaxation/preparation section. Familiar words help participants to unwind and find a safe place from which to embark. Any repetition is, therefore, intentional and is reprinted on each meditation to eliminate flipping back and forth in the book during the meditation section of the session.

After the relaxation/preparation section, I normally begin by grounding the meditators in a place that is safe for them. Sometimes I will suggest a safe place that is connected with the meditation. Sometimes, they are invited to imagine themselves in a place that is safe and comfortable for them. This may be a place they know, or it may be a place they create in their imagination. If there are very deeply wounded people in your group, don't be surprised if they have a lot of difficulty with this. Tragically, there are people who have never in all their lives experienced a place where they felt safe. Gently remind participants that they can create one for themselves and return to it whenever they choose.

To be really grounded imaginatively means using all the senses—getting a sense of the colours, of the smells, of the sounds, of the textures, of the feeling of sun or breeze on the skin.

At the end of the meditation it is important to return to the same place from which one began, and to be there for a few seconds before being gradually and gently brought back to the group, back to awareness of breath and body-self.

At the end of a meditation, a period of silence is needed to ground the meditation, to let it take root in consciousness. Some will want to journal or draw at this time. It is a time to move from what happened inside, during meditation, to prepare to share the experience with others. This takes a few moments.

Language for the Holy Presence

For leading meditations, I have found Carolyn Stahl's advice on language about God and Christ to be very helpful.[5] The more open the symbol, the more it evokes. When I am doing a meditation specifically around the historical Jesus, I may refer to "Jesus," but often I find that the term "the Christ" evokes something broader than the historical person. In our group experience "Christ" has come in images both male and female, as a child, as healing light, as living water, as a gardener, as a vine, as a particular person in whom a meditator has experienced Christ-presence, or as an awareness of presence, of power, of energy, but not necessarily as an image. By being too concrete in imaging the Holy, we can block God's Spirit from manifesting itself in the way the Spirit desires. We can lock God or Christ imagery into such tight boxes, that God doesn't get a chance to come to us in the way God wants, or in the way we are able to receive.

I never cease to be amazed by the versatility and ingenuity of the Spirit in the ways it breaks through to various individuals. And it never ceases to move me how totally appropriate the particular image is for the meditator. As a pastor, I am often privy to deep personal issues in the lives of those in the group. It is nothing short of miraculous to watch the God who finds exactly the right way to reach each person.

I have found that the word "God" sometimes carries a lot of baggage in people's histories and unfortunately often evokes an image of a rigid, judgmental, uncaring presence. There are others who need to hear the more traditional language in order to feel safe in meditation.

When I have a lot of people in recovery in the group, I use the term "Higher Power" several times, so that they can connect that familiar concept to the Holy of which I am speaking. I think most of us in the church would do well to reflect on Moses' encounter with the burning bush where *The Name* was given. It is an almost untranslatable *I am who I am, I will be who I will be, I am being-ness becoming*; not exactly a concrete image one can "nail down." Yet even this ineffable name was considered to be so sacred that it could not be spoken. Other words that stood for the unspeakable *Name* were used (i.e. words that have been translated as "Lord").

Jesus, in trying to show that this holy reality was not only other-ness and far away, used the term *abba*. This was shocking at the time, because it was an intimate term of family endearment, "dadda." Jesus knew that God was more than the images that had been used up to that time.

I use God imagery that is as open and as symbolic as possible. I also use a wide variety of words. In this way I hope I am letting God fill in the spaces. The Holy Presence comes with freedom in the way it desires and chooses.

Letting Flow

It is important to *let be* in meditation. Do not try to force images, or use meditation as a means to an end. Meditation itself is worthwhile, whether it yields any deep wisdom or not. Expectations of how or what one *should* see only block the process. Just concentrate on the visual journey and let it take you where it will. Do not censor images that you cannot understand or that do not seem "holy." What is needed is an attitude of waiting upon the presence of the Spirit.

In the meditation, often I will suggest that the person bring a gift to the Holy Presence (allowing space for that to emerge as it will), and that they receive a gift from the Sacred One. This is a way of grounding the meditation and bridging the inner experience of the visualization and the conscious, everyday reality of one's life.

Making Sense of Images and Symbols

Certain images have fairly widespread symbolic meaning. In most bookstores and libraries there are dictionaries of symbols.[6] The following are fairly widely accepted interpretations:

- **Water imagery** usually is connected with the unconscious. If it is a river, it may connect with the flow of one's life and the flow of energy or of feelings.
- **Butterflies** often symbolize transformation, resurrection.
- **Houses or buildings** usually have something to do with the self and with how one experiences the self. The basement moves deeper into the unconscious, the rooftop the connection with the Divine.
- **Paths and roads** usually connect with one's life course, and have something to say about how we are experiencing that journey.
- **Seeds, plants, trees** have to do with growth, or some aspect of growth.
- **A baby** often means a new thing that is being born in your life, a part of you that is still new and vulnerable, but which has great potential for growth.
- **A wise person** often means wisdom or inner guidance. Sometimes this person is the mediator between God and the self.
- **The moon** usually represents female sacred energy and the tugging power that creates ebb and flow. It may represent a gentle wisdom-light in the darkness.
- **The sun** may represent male sacred energy, energy for action, for growth, for warmth.

While these are some fairly widespread understandings of symbols, when a symbol emerges it does so in the particular context of a person's life and so the same symbol may have different meanings for different people. It is important not to be too rigid with interpretations.

Images may relate to various levels of meaning, both in dreams and in meditation. The image may be about something directly connected with one's external world. Or it may connect with inner reality and with the processes, emotional and spiritual, that are happening within. Sometimes the images work on a variety of levels at once. The experience of running up against an invisible wall of resistance on a journey may refer to some roadblock in the outer world. It may connect with inner barriers, or it may symbolize resistance that must be faced and named.

What happens in meditation may be very subtle—nothing nameable, not an image, not a phrase, not a feeling even—but a profound knowing that is transformative. The meditator enters a process of the death of the ego, so that the higher self, the God-self, can become more rooted in the meditator. In the losing, in the letting go, one finds a treasure of great price, a more complete self, more compassionate, connected, differentiated, joy-filled, courageous, grounded, passionate, creative, free. These qualities will be recognized as qualities that are very present in Jesus.

It is this process of transformation that I believe scripture is talking about when it speaks of losing the self, but gaining the whole world. It is what mystics have spoken of for centuries; this vast expansion of being that happens when the small-self is released. Jesus spoke of being born again and of entering the reign of God. But this often happens in subtle ways, like the planting of a mustard seed or the tiny, unseen yeast in the dough.

Meditations are not something used once then thrown aside. The same meditation can be done over and over again. Each time the meditator is a different person experiencing the meditation; so there is always the possibility of a "new thing" arising. As well, when you find a particular meditation that speaks deeply to you, it is good to go into it again; perhaps to place yourself in the scene in a different way in order to experience more levels of the meditation. Feeling, listening, observing what is happening in the meditation, and noticing how it is affecting you is a process that can be repeated over and over, with new insights gained.

I have a particular meditation called The Healing Pool from my previous book, *The Healing Oasis*. This meditation speaks deeply to me. Whenever I begin meditation and go to a safe place, this is most often where I will go. After years with this image, I find I can enter it quite quickly and go to the familiar place, and a sense of calm, of inner peace, of well-being comes over me almost immediately when I picture it in my mind's eye. It keeps unfolding new truth and insight, and in this place I meet the Holy often.

Silence for Grounding the Meditation

At the end of meditation, it is good to leave a period of silence, with the music playing, before beginning to speak. This is an important transition time between the inner experience and sharing that experience with others. A bell might be used to break the silence.

Sharing

The sharing segment of each meditation includes two basic sections: silence for journalling and debriefing. Specific suggestions appear with each meditation, but keep the following general suggestions in mind for each session.

Some participants find it helpful to ground their experience by journalling. Give space to those who wish to write down or draw their insights. Ask them to note any particular image, word, phrase, feeling, understanding that came to them. Encourage participants to ask themselves the question, "What does this experience mean for my life?" They may or may not share this writing with others.

After silence and journalling, invite the participants to share what they wish from their meditation. Allow participants to share as they feel moved, rather than going around the circle. Groups of seven or under are best for sharing meditation experiences. When we have had large groups, we have divided into smaller groups for sharing.

Sharing the experience soon after having it helps to ground the experience in consciousness and to listen for its meaning. I have often said in our groups that by sharing and honouring our spiritual experience we resist the culture's devaluation of the spiritual, of intuition, of imagination, of feeling, and of experience. To have one's sacred experience witnessed helps the meditator to integrate it more fully. For those who have the privilege of listening, it can also bring spiritual wealth and wisdom. Sharing of spiritual experience is one of the greatest gifts we can offer to one another.

As a leader, at this stage of the session, I am listening particularly for what God has been doing in the meditation. I try to lift up the meditator's own experience of God for the person to see and to savour, so that it can take root more deeply. We have one group member who is quite shy. When the Spirit gives him a particular insight, it is usually in the form of a message or a gift, but he has a tendency to skip over it very quickly when he talks about it. I repeat back the words that he has been given, mirror them back to him, and help him to integrate the gift. In this way I help him to receive and reinforce the power of his experience. This is the type of response that is most useful in sharing, rather than moving into analyzing and intellectualizing.

When just out of a meditation, meditators are very vulnerable and open. They have lowered their barriers. Their holy ground must be approached with great respect, "with our shoes removed" so to speak. A good rule is that we are to hear one another's experience, to witness it, to receive it as a sacred gift. Our role is to help each other savour and honour the experience. We are not there to analyze, to problem solve, or to fix one another. Without this fundamental attitude, an atmosphere of safety is not created.

A meditation is not good or bad in itself. Its meaning cannot be abstracted from the context in which it was experienced, which is the life-journey of the meditator. Therefore it is very dangerous, and presumptuous, for others to assume that they are better placed to understand the meaning of a meditation than the meditator herself or himself.

As with dreams, beware the interpretations of others, beware allegorical explanations, beware literal interpretations. Most problems and tensions have arisen in our group when one group member tried to interpret another's meditation through her or his own filters. This can have the effect of stealing the experience from the one who had it, or of putting the experience into an inappropriate box.

It can be helpful for others to suggest what the story evokes for them. This gives the fellow meditator the opportunity to connect with each insight or not, as feels appropriate. Questions to help clarify or to open up the telling of the story can also be helpful, as long as they do not probe too much. Permission needs to be explicitly given so that the person sharing her or his experience can ask the questioner to stop at any time. The leader needs to be the gatekeeper, especially if the person sharing the meditation is not very assertive.

Those with the most positive experiences will usually share first. Someone who feels that the experience is negative, or that "nothing has happened" often holds back, unsure if it is safe to share. The first person who shares such an experience gives the group a great gift because it creates safety for others to be completely real with their own experience.

Meditation is not a failure if you do not hear bells ringing and have no Technicolour movies rolling. When someone tells me that "nothing happened," I ask them to tell me about that "nothing." Often in what one thought was "nothing," there can be insight about what was blocking or what was causing resistance. Sometimes the "nothing" holds feelings of alienation or fear of feeling. This, in itself, can be the spiritual insight the Spirit is offering. Accepting what is, trying to discern the meaning of all experience, is a necessary attitude. There are no fixed rules around experience that participants are supposed to *obey.*

We need to cultivate wisdom and grounded-ness in reflecting on the meditations in order to distinguish truth from illusion. We need to be able to distinguish the results of mind-chatter from deep, spiritual wisdom, and to practise reliable thinking about meditation. Reality in meditations does not obey the same rules as reality in daily life. It has more of a dream-reality quality—very profound in its power to heal, give wisdom, and even insight and direction to one's life, but not to be taken literally and acted on in a literal fashion. We know that some dreams have great power, wisdom, and truth; while some are just the unconscious processing of last night's movie or some experience you have just had. Discernment of meaning is important.

The most negative experiences in groups I have been associated with have been with the very few people who felt that they needed to *produce,* week after week, cosmic, transformative meditations. This kind of spiritual grandstanding shows real insecurity. The participant's actual experience is not felt to be adequate so he or she manufactures an experience in order to have status in the group. The tragedy is that, until this attitude changes, a spiritual lie is created and that insulates the meditator from the genuine experience he or she so deeply desires.

It is important for a leader to be able to confront this gently if it is happening. I have done this by talking about how we know when something is a "real" experience and when it is just from our mind-chatter, conscious, ego part of our psyche. The participants can inevitably come up with a list that helps us all become more conscious and more critical (in a good sense) of the experiences we hear. It is easy to recognize the difference in quality and in feeling between genuine experience and encounter and experience that is generated out of ego needs.

Genuine experience has a palpable feeling of integrity. It comes with surprise, usually, because it is not what the meditator expected. It is rooted in relationship with God, and is not just talking about what the person thinks God might feel or think. It has a transformational quality to it that speaks to the soul of the person. The listener senses that it comes from the very core, and so it has authority. Often tears accompany it, or some other emotional reaction. It is also congruent with the experience of God that we know through Christ.

It is important that times of spiritual dryness be acknowledged, and even honoured, as an important part of the spiritual journey. There are desert periods on the spiritual journey. We might feel God is completely absent and that our lives are going in circles. We might not even be able to see where God is providing manna and water because this nurture comes in unfamiliar places. Experiences that are interpreted as negative need to be talked about and examined. This creates trust in a group and the permission to be real. This is vital for the healthy life of the group.

If a person has not shared at the end of the group, I ask if there is anyone else who would like to share before we draw the group to an end. In this way there is no pressure to share, but no one is cut off by unexpected closure.

Sometimes it is helpful to share the meditation with a trusted friend or spiritual guide, a minister or spiritual director, as well as sharing with the group. I am sometimes concerned about those who do not share with anyone in order to help them process the experience. The leader needs to be available after the group for at least one half-hour in case there is someone who needs to talk privately, or there are those who want to make appointments for another time. Often this will not be necessary, but it is good to be aware that it may be needed.

Closure

This is usually a very brief part of the session. Often I will ask participants to reflect on how they saw God "being" for them in their meditation, and to call out the one or two words that best describe this. It is amazing to hear words like comforting, challenging, showing, encouraging, clarifying, reminding, healing, unsettling, disturbing, being absent, stirring up, inviting, connecting, and so many more. We know we have experienced a Presence that is active and alive in our times and in our lives.

At other times I ask participants to look around the circle to see the face of God in each one present, and to offer blessing and peace to one another. I invite participants to remember these faces during the week, and the stories they have shared in this gathering, and to hold one another in the Spirit in the following week.

A closure may include a particular ritual e.g. using water, or salt, or light, or the sharing of seeds or stones. Where something specific seems appropriate, I have suggested it in the meditation itself. The following three general closing rituals are appropriate for many meditations.

1. A Body Blessing

Stand in a circle. Explain the movements slowly and prayerfully. I have found that it works best if only the person leading has the words. This helps those praying to focus on praying the body itself, rather than on trying to read words. You may wish to have copies available for participants to take home so that they can integrate this prayer into their personal prayer time.

When there are persons with physical disabilities in the group, it is important to be sensitive to their needs. In such circumstances, the blessing might be introduced with an acknowledgement that it is a group with differing physical abilities, and we can celebrate and bless the bodies we have. Where people are not able to do the actions, you could suggest that they do what they can and allow their imagination to help with the rest of the action.

Honouring that which is most Holy,

(*Hands together in prayer mode in front of the heart.*)

Accept from me,

(*Gradually open hands and raise arms above head in prayer gesture.*)

The Spirit of my Soul.

(*Bring hands facing forward together over head so that the little fingers link together. This forms a kind of butterfly or spirit symbol. Draw this "butterfly" down to the heart as you say "soul."*)

I place it in this vessel,

(*Hands come down to abdominal level and form a cup container. Feel the weight of the offering it contains.*)

And offer it up.

(*Raise the hand container slowly and intentionally above the head as an offering to God.*)

Pour down your gentle blessing upon me,

(*Open hands, turn palms towards you as you move fingers in a rain-like movement down to your shoulders.*)

As I stand before you with an open heart.

(*Open hands, palms forward, moved to sides at shoulder level, in an attitude of surrender and openness.*)

Bless my mind that it may think with clarity and wisdom.

(Hands touch the head.)

Bless my eyes that they may see beauty and truth around me.

(Touch eyes.)

Bless my ears that they may hear the pain and joy of life.

(Touch ears.)

Bless my mouth that I may speak your truth.

(Touch mouth.)

Bless my heart that I may have the passion and compassion to respond.

(Touch heart.)

Bless my whole body that it may be a temple of your Spirit.

(One hand on heart, another on abdomen.)

Bless my hands that they may touch life with tenderness and healing.

(Open hands.)

Bless my feet that they may root me to the earth and carry me where you would have me go.

(Reach out towards feet, not necessarily touching them.)

Bless my soul that it may always join me to your love and to the world

you created and love.

(Raise hands in a straight line through the centre of the body above the head, then open them outwards to make a circle as you say the words. Reach out to take the hand of the person on either side of you as the last line is spoken.)

2. Exchange of Peace

We often close by offering peace to one another. It is important to remind the group that there are those who need and love hugs, and there are those who are not at all comfortable with them. We always need to ask permission to hug. Many women who have been abused by men and who have come to the group unable to tolerate any physical contact with a man, have met loving, caring, nurturing, vulnerable men in our groups and have been able to receive and to ask for hugs for the first time in their lives. The freedom to refuse to be touched is part of what helps to make acceptance on a future occasion possible. It is also important to remind the group that while some believe a firm handshake is a sign of character, others with arthritis, osteoporosis, etc. cannot stand the pressure of a firm handshake.

3. Closure Song

Sometimes it is appropriate to sing a closure. This depends upon your group's size and comfort with singing. It also depends upon the mood of the group at the end of the gathering. There are many songs that are useful for closure. Some specific suggestions are made with individual mediations. Here are some general suggestions from *Voices United.*

- "Stay with Us through the Night" (#182)
- "Amazing Grace" (#266)
- "Come and Find the Quiet Centre" (#374)
- "Spirit of the Living God" (#376)
- "Spirit of Life" (#381)
- "Breathe on Me, Breath of God" (#382)
- "The Lone, Wild Bird" (selected verses) (#384)
- "God Is Passionate Life" (adding healing or other appropriate words) (#695)
- "May the Blessing of God Go before You" (#962)
- "Go Now in Peace" (#964)
- "The Lord Bless Thee, and Keep Thee" (#965)

Part II

Meditations for All Seasons

MEDITATION

1

In the Palm of God's Hand

Resting in God's Presence

Introduction

Preparation

- music, such as "I will never forget you my people" sung by the St. Louis Jesuits (in *Glory and Praise*; see Endnote 13) and the sung response to Psalm 62 "Rest in God alone" (*Voices United* #779) may be used at the beginning or the end of the session
- paper and pens for journalling
- CD player and appropriate background music
- worship centre with candle, images of hands and of a baby or child being cradled by an older person
- bell to ring when shifting from writing to meditation

Scripture

Isaiah 49:15–16

Reflection

Letting go and trusting Sacred Presence is a lifelong challenge. There are times when we find it easy to relax into the flow of God's presence. There are other times when our "questioning, critical" voice will be so present that it becomes almost impossible to "let go and let God."

Questions arise, such as "Who do I think I am to believe God cares about me?" or "What is the use of doing this?" or "Am I really just imagining this experience is from God?" Paying attention to this critical voice will rob us of deep, spiritual experience. I find that it helps to notice this voice, to thank it for trying to help you, but to tell this voice that it is not helping right now and that you need to be free to trust what you are doing. You may be amazed by the response you get from your critical self.

This meditation uses the image of being carved in the palm of God's hand. The scripture uses powerful imagery as it asks: "Can a loving mother forget the child of her womb or the infant at her breast?" Anyone who has experienced giving birth and nursing a child can connect with the powerful bond that forms between mother and child. Yet Isaiah's God says, "Even these may forget [and that is almost impossible], yet I will not forget you."

Gathering (Choose a, b, or c)

a) Look at your hands.
Remember all the things you have done with your hands this past week. Remember all the people your hands have touched. Remember hands that have touched you with love when you were a young child; hands that were rough and worn by weather and hard work; hands that were gentle and soft; hands that held you when you were sad or frightened; hands that helped you up when you had fallen; hands that held yours in love; hands that healed you when you were ill. Share with the group.

b) Isaiah chooses imagery of the birthing, nursing mother as a metaphor for God's compassionate, passionate love. What memories, experiences, challenges, or connections does that metaphor hold for you?

c) You may wish to play the song "I will never forget you my people" or sing the chant from Psalm 62 "Rest in God Alone" (*Voices United* #779).

Meditation

Sit quietly in an upright position.

Close your eyes ... Become aware of this body-self that is you, as you come to meditation today ... Focus on your breath ... Notice the pattern of your breathing ... as it moves in ... as it moves out ... Follow your breath in ... Follow your breath out ... Notice how fast you are breathing ... Notice whether you are breathing deeply or with shallow breaths ... Notice where your body moves when you breathe ... Is the movement in your chest ... or in your belly? ...

Watch your breathing for a few minutes ... notice any changes that occur ... You may find that just attending to your breath will allow you to relax ... As you focus and breathe let your breaths become slower and deeper ... Let your body relax and move to a place of peace ...

Notice where your body is sore or tense ... Imagine the breath moving to that place ... and gently massaging the tightened knots of tension ... or fear ... or anger ... or stress ... Simply allow the breath to open up your body ... so that your life energy can flow freely ... You are preparing yourself for prayer.

As you focus on your breathing ... you may notice thoughts coming and going ... Just notice the thoughts ... and then let them go ... You may want to imagine them as clouds floating across the horizon ... or as leaves on a stream being carried away ... As thoughts arise ... gently return your focus to your breath ... Notice the space that opens inside you as you relax ... as you gradually come into your sacred centre ...

Ask God to bless this meditation journey and to use it for your highest good of mind ... body ... and spirit ...

In your mind's eye, I invite you to imagine that you are in a safe and sacred place ... It is a place that you may choose from your past experience ... or a place you create in your imagination ... Be in touch with the place you have chosen ... Notice the colours ... the textures ... the odours ... the whole feel of the place you have chosen ... Notice if you are alone in that place or whether others are there ...

Once you are deeply connected with this sacred place ... there arises in you a knowing that you have been invited here by the Spirit ... that the God in whom you live ... and move ... and have your being ... flows through this place with deep, unconditional love for you ... Take some time to be in touch with this Source of Love ...

Notice the feelings that arise in you as you are invited to encounter the Spirit ... Notice how the Spirit comes to you ... Does it have form? ... Is it a feeling? ... Is it a knowing? ... Simply allow the Holy to be with you in whatever way the Spirit comes to you today ... Experience the words from the Spirit ... "I remember you ... I know you from before you were born ... I have always known you ... I could never forget you ... I love you more than a new mother her child ...You are mine ...You are inscribed on the palm of my hands ... Rest there ... Let me hold you in the palm of my hand."

Allow yourself to let go ... to be held up and supported by God ... You may wish to imagine it as being held in the palm of God's hand ... or it may come as another image ...

Be in this safe space where you are known by your Creator ...

As you rest in God ... notice your soul coming home ...

As you rest in God ... feel what it is like to be known to the core by Ultimate Love ...

As you rest in God ... feel the stresses, the distractions of your life fall away ... for you know what is important ... what is real ... what matters ...

As you rest in God ... feel the fears and anxiety you carry fall away ...

As you rest in God ... feel the anger and pain you carry fall away ...

As you rest in God ... feel the healing power of the Creator flowing through you ... and around you ... filling you with sacred light ... healing light ...

As you rest in God ... know that you can live your life rooted in that love ... in the knowing that you are loved ... that you are known by name by your Creator ... that you are precious to God ...

Notice if there is anything the Spirit would like to say to you as you rest in God's presence ...

When you feel ready ... gradually draw yourself back to this place ... Notice your breath ... notice your body-self as it is sitting in the chair ... Feel the bottom of your feet as they connect you with the earth ... Gradually make some gentle movements with your toes and fingers ... some circles with your shoulders and head ... When you are ready open your eyes ...

Silence

Provide an opportunity for journalling for those who wish.

Ring the bell at the end of the silent time to call people into the group again.

Debriefing

- How was God with you in your meditation today?
- What did you experience?

Closure

If you did not use one of the pieces of music suggested in Gathering on page 34, you might use it as closure.

MEDITATION

2

The Island

Preparing Space for Prayer

Introduction

Preparation

- paper and pens for journalling
- CD player with appropriate background music
- worship centre for the circle with cloth, candle, open Bible, bowl of water, and other symbols that reflect peace and tranquility
- bell to ring when shifting from writing to meditation

Scripture (Choose one reading)

Psalm 61:1–2, Psalm 141:2, Matthew 6:5–6, Philippians 1:9–10

Reflection

Prayer is relationship with God. How we image or understand God has a major impact on how we understand and experience prayer.

In childhood, my image of God was of an all-powerful, up-there king in the sky. So I prayed expecting God to intervene on my behalf to meet my wishes, which I perceived often as needs.

When I was a teenager, the image I had of a theistic, out-there God died. I could no longer pray to God as a divine bellhop in the sky and then wonder why God did not answer my prayer. I thought God had died as did many others at that time. It felt devastating.

I discovered that this was just the beginning of a new journey with the Spirit. In order for God to break free of the box in which my images limited God, those images had to break down. Letting God go free; searching and questioning; and letting God be who God would be opened me to a deeper experience of God as a living Source of all that is. I came to know through experience, as well as in my thinking processes, the One in whom I live and move and have my being. (Acts 17:28) I experienced God as the living Spirit who moves in and through all of creation, including me.

This journey involved a powerful, mystical experience at the birth of a child. It then deepened while I was working as a potter for nine years, recognizing the symbolism of what emerged from the creative process as the leading of the Spirit. It involved intellectual searching and reading of newer theology. It involved learning to trust my own experience of the Holy rather than believing that I had to learn everything second-hand through the "experts." These experts did not always use language or metaphor that spoke to my experience.

With this evolving sense of who God was, prayer had to change for me. I had to learn paths that could help me open to this Sacred Presence. I had to learn ways to listen for the Spirit as it moved through my own life and through the life of the world. Learning to slow down (an ongoing struggle), to relax and shift gears from being engaged in the outer world, and to take time to be contemplative, reflective, and meditative helped me to deepen into God's presence in my life.

As I opened to God, it helped me connect with the divine presence both in the lives of those I met and in the passion and pain of the world. So contemplative time, rather than being an escape from the world, has actually been a deepening of being that awakened me to God's call in the world.

Only as I started to practise meditation and contemplative prayer did I start to notice all the times in the gospels where they spoke of Jesus going to pray after particularly testing, exhausting times. They also spoke of him returning from prayer to engage in his healing, justice-making ministry. That rhythm and balance of action and meditation has become very important to me.

This meditation uses the imagery of an island as a way of moving deeper and deeper to centre and connect with the Heart of Love.

Gathering **(Choose a or b)**

a) How do you pray? What is your understanding of prayer and how it works?

b) When you think of the word "island," what image, thought, or memory comes to mind?

Meditation

Close your eyes ... Become aware of this body-self that is you, as you come to meditation today ... Focus on your breath ... Notice the pattern of your breathing ... as it moves in ... as it moves out ... Follow your breath in ... Follow your breath out ... Notice how fast you are breathing ... Notice whether you are breathing deeply or with shallow breaths ... Notice where your body moves when you breathe ... Is the movement in your chest ... or in your belly? ...

Watch your breathing for a few minutes ... notice any changes that occur ... You may find that just attending to your breath allows you to relax ... As you focus and breathe, let your breaths become slower and deeper ... Let your body relax and move to a place of peace ...

If you notice places where your body is sore or tense ... imagine the breath moving to that place ... and gently massaging the tightened knots of tension ... or fear ... or anger ... or stress ... Simply allow the breath to open up your body ... so that your life energy can flow freely ... You are preparing yourself for prayer...

As you focus on your breathing ... you may notice thoughts coming and going ... Just notice the thoughts ... then let them go ... You may want to imagine them as clouds floating across the horizon ... or as leaves on a stream being carried away ... As thoughts arise ... gently return your focus to your breath ... Notice the space that opens inside you as you relax ... as you gradually come into your sacred centre ...

Ask God to bless this meditation journey and use it for the highest good of your mind ... body ... and spirit ...

In your mind's eye ... imagine that you are on the shore looking at an island several kilometres across ... You sense as you look at this island that it is a holy place ... The desire to go there rises up in you ...

You notice a bridge that joins this island with the mainland ... and you walk across it ... As you walk over the bridge ... you notice the clouds reflected in the water ... and the breeze that gently caresses the smooth surface ...

You arrive on the island and feel that this is a peaceful place ... a sacred place ... a place that is safe ... There are no people there ... The sun is shining ... and the clouds are beautiful and white against the deep blue sky... Feel the warmth of the sun on your skin ... Feel the comfortable and very gentle breeze that cools you down in the sun ... Notice the trees and bushes ... the wild flowers ... the birds ... the colours ... the sounds ... the smells of this place ...

Enjoy the beauty of this place of solitude ... See the dappled sun on the grass ... See how the breeze lightly blows through the grass and the leaves of the trees ... All is calm ... but in motion ... The wind blows ... the sun moves across the sky ... birds fly ... and you walk easily through the beauty of this scene ... This is indeed God's sacred world ...

You notice a path that leads you to the centre of the island ... You come to a large flat stone on a slight hillock ... You sit down ... allowing a deeper sense of peace to fill you ... You are safe and comfortable in a beautiful place ... As you sit ... close your eyes and feel connected with the rock on which you are seated ... feel connected with this ancient stone ... that has arisen from the heart of the earth ... Feel a part of this place ... completely at home with the natural world ... Know that this is a sacred place where you can look deep inside and feel perfectly safe ...

As you turn your attention to your inner world ... notice your heart ... Notice the light of Christ present with you in your heart ... This light may be dim at first ... but as you focus on it ... the light grows ... See this light clearly ... and gradually let it spread throughout your body ... Every part of your body becomes illuminated from inside ... And as this light fills you ... you notice that the light is not translucent but clear ... It shines into every cell of your body ... bringing vitality ... health ... a strong sense of being loved ... being connected with your source ...

Let this light pour through your mind and thought patterns ... Let it illuminate and heal your memories ... Let it clear away anything that you can let go of at this time ...

Let it move through your emotional life ... bringing its clarifying, healing energy ... Let it clear away anything that can be let go of at this time ...

Allow the love and light of Christ to illuminate your experience ... Allow the peace of Christ to help you understand the power of love and to know your heart ...

Say to yourself ... "May I be energized by the light of Christ's love" ... "May I grow in wisdom" ... "May I find peace in my heart of compassion" ... "May I live in the full light of God's love."

Stay with this healing Christ light in your heart ... enjoying its beauty ...

When you are ready, gradually move from the rock ... and walk across the island to the bridge that brings you to the place where you began ... Know that you can return to this peaceful, beautiful place in your heart any time you desire ... You can use this experience to energize your body ... your mind ... your spirit ... to reconnect with the essence of love that is your core ...

When you are ready, clench your fists ... make some gentle movements with your toes ... your neck ... open your eyes and stretch your muscles ...

Silence

Provide a time for journalling or drawing for those who find it helpful.

Ring the bell at the end of the silent time to call people into the group again.

Debriefing

Invite participants to share their experience of meditation.

Closure

In the centre of the circle, invite participants to say words or phrases that describe how they experienced God being with them or with the group during this session.

Gather the prayer in your own words or in the Lord's Prayer.

MEDITATION

3

The Tree of Life

Opening to the Flow of Life in Your Body, Mind, and Spirit

Introduction

This is a good meditation for personal health and well-being or for opening the body for healing work.

Preparation

- worship centre with photos of trees in all seasons, and a plant, such as a bonsai
- paper/pens and crayons for drawing or journalling
- CD player with appropriate background music
- scriptures that best meet the needs of the group or that introduce the prevalence of the image
- bell to ring when shifting from writing to meditation

Scripture

Psalm 1, Genesis 2:8—3:7, Revelation 22:1-2

Trees are mentioned in each of these scripture readings. Psalm 1: They shall be like a tree planted beside a river that bears fruit in the right time. Genesis 2:8—3:7: The tree of the knowledge of good and evil. Revelation 22:1-2: The trees on each side of the river of life that bear fruit for the healing of the nations.

Reflection

Scripture is full of tree imagery. The second creation story in Genesis 2 revolves around the tree of life and the tree of the knowledge of good and evil. Many scholars see this as an ancient story about humanity coming out of illusion into consciousness. The fruit of the tree is the vehicle for gaining wisdom and for transformation. One can also see the tree of the knowledge of good and evil as the beginning of our human tendency to divide life into dualities. Perhaps this ancient story is an attempt to explain our tendency to "either–or" thinking. In contrast, there is unity in the tree of life.

As in the beginning, so in the end, there is a tree of life. We read of it in the final vision of John of Patmos in Revelation. Here the holy city contains the image of the river with the water of life flowing through its centre. One can only imagine what our cities would be like with the river of "the water of life" flowing at their heart and centre!

On either side of this river stands the tree of life, which yields 12 crops—one for each month of the year—and whose leaves are for the healing of the nations. How we long for that vision of wholeness and healing—healing for all seasons! It seems the scripture is clearly telling us of the Creator's intention for healing and for life in all its fullness.

Like human beings, trees act as a link between heaven and earth. The image of the tree with roots growing deep into the earth and branches reaching out to the cosmos has become an important image to connect me with the sacred life that flows through me. When I do this meditation, as I have done for years, it helps the energies in my body to flow freely and enables me to root myself in the earth and connect with the sacred energy of the cosmos.

This helpful image prepares for laying on of hands in healing touch or simply to feel one's connectedness to the universe and to the sacred energy that flows through it. It is used in the Healing Pathway[7] program to prepare practitioners to heal. It opens one to the life energy of the Creator, in whom we live and move and have our being.

Gathering (Choose a, b, c, or d)

a) Invite group members to remember a favourite tree and to share why it is their favourite.

b) Invite group members to reflect on the image of the tree.

If they were to imagine themselves as a tree, in what season would they find themselves? Share around the circle or in manageable, smaller groups.

c) Read Revelation 22:1–2.

When you image the river of life flowing through the city and the tree of life on either side, what comes to mind? If God's life were flowing through your "city," what might that look like?

d) Invite group members to have their journals handy to write down or draw any reaction or insight they might have gathered from the meditation.

Meditation

Close your eyes ... Notice what it feels like to be in this body-self that is you right now ... Most of us go through whole days, whole lives, without paying attention to this body-self ... In Hebrew (the language system Jesus knew), there was no such thing as disembodied spirit ... They spoke of the *nephesh*...the body soul...the spirit body ... Jesus talked about our bodies as temples of the Spirit ... What is it like for you to think of yourself in that way? ...

As you begin to pay attention to your body, do you notice places where tension is stored up ... places where your muscles are in tight knots? ... As you scan your body ... from the top of your head to the bottom of your feet ... notice if there are tender places ... and send compassion to these places in your body ... thank them for the hard work they are doing ... You might offer to pay more attention to what they are telling you in the future ...

Become aware of your breathing ... this life-giving process that goes on all the time ... even when we are not conscious of it ... Notice if you are breathing with only a small part of your lungs ... or whether you are taking the breath deeply into your whole being ... down to the bottom of your lungs ... up to the tops of your shoulders ... Notice if your tummy moves in and out as you inhale and exhale ... This is how a baby breathes when it is breathing naturally ... before its body has become tense and locked up with the stress of living ...

When we do not breathe fully ... we are not fully open to the breath of life ... Let your body relax ... Let the tension flow out of your body through your feet ... Begin to allow your breath to move more deeply into your being ...

Take the breath deep down into your belly ... Breathe in deeply the healing presence of God ... the goodness and grace of God ... Take it right into the core of your being ... As you breathe out ... let the breath carry with it the poisons ... physical ... emotional ... spiritual that have built up in your system ... Breathe in the newness of possibility ... Breathe in the hope that God gives ... Let go of the stress and tensions that are stored in your body-self ... in your emotional self ... in your spiritual self ... Breathe in life energy ... the creating breath of God that was there from the beginning ... Breathe out whatever blocks you from being fully present to this time ...

Again notice your body ... If there are still tense places, imagine this healing breath moving directly to those spots ... loosening the tension ... letting go ... letting be ... opening ... unlocking ...

Know that you are in a safe place ... Notice the inner space that is being prepared and opened up inside you ... space for the Sacred Presence to find room ... space for the Holy One to be with you ... your own sacred space ...your own holy ground ...

In that place, I invite you to imagine yourself as a tree ... What kind of tree are you? ... How tall are you? ... How healthy is your growth? ... Be in touch with the texture of your trunk ... and how your branches spread out into the sky ...

Imagine your roots going down deeply into the soil ... Feel your feet opening as the roots go deep down into the earth, drawing up what you need from the earth ... Feel the goodness of the earth ... the energy of the earth coming into your roots ... drawing up into your feet ... Notice if this energy has a colour ...

Feel it rise in your strong trunk ... bringing life as it moves through your ankles ... your legs ... your torso ... down through your arms ... and up through the top of your head ... Imagine your trunk strong, rising to the sky ... carrying this nurture to the branches ...

Now bring awareness to your branches ... Are there many of them? ... Be in touch with these branches as they reach out to the cosmos ... Imagine them reaching up and drawing in the sacred energy of the sky ... drawing in the sacred energy of the sun ... of the air ... of the rain ... of the whole cosmos beyond this earth ... Imagine this as sacred white healing light ... light of the Creator ... light of Christ flowing into you ... bringing you the energy and life of the Creator ... Feel the profound love that comes in this light ...

Allow this energy to flow into your body through the top of your head ... filling your mind and your thinking ... your eyes and your seeing ... your ears and your hearing ... your mouth and your speaking ... Feel it moving through your throat ... awakening your voice and your creativity ... moving into your heart ... opening your heart space ... filling it with holy love ... Imagine it flowing through your whole body ... as it connects with and dances with the energy you have drawn up from the earth ...

Feel the dance of life in you ... Feel the tree of life rooted deep in the earth ... linking earth and sky ... reaching to the stars ... connecting with the presence of God that flows through you and through all of creation ... Allow this flow of life to balance your mind ... your body ... and your spirit ... Allow this flow of life to enliven and to heal your mind ... your body ... and your spirit ... Take some time to bathe in this healing flow of spirit ... Allow this flow of life ... this flow of love to pour through you as you touch your world with healing ...

Gradually draw yourself back to this place ... knowing that as you do so ... you stay connected with this flow of life ...

Silence

Provide a time for journalling or drawing for those in the group who find this helpful.

Ring the bell at the end of the silent time to call people into the group again.

Debriefing

What did you experience as you did this meditation?

Closure

Here is an opportunity for healing touch if you feel it is appropriate for your group.

In some groups or retreat settings, I have led this meditation and then invited people to work in pairs, one seated, the other standing behind the chair. (I am assuming the group is already sitting in a circle so this continues to be a circle with every second chair empty.) The person standing places hands on the shoulders of the person seated and images the flow of healing, loving energy moving out of his or her hands into the other person. Offer healing presence and allow the love of Christ to flow through you. Continue for three to five minutes then share how it was for each of you. Reverse roles and repeat.

In the Healing Pathway program, this is called "Soaking Prayer." It can be a very useful and simple tool for pastoral caregivers when this kind of touch and silent prayer is appropriate.

When I offer it in pastoral care situations, I will often pray extemporaneously as I am offering it, that the light of Christ might fill (*Name*) with healing, with love, with compassion, with forgiveness, with strength, with whatever it appears that the person particularly needs at this time.

MEDITATION

4

The Seasons of Our Lives

Introduction

Preparation

- worship centre with photos of trees in all seasons, and a plant, such as a bonsai
- paper/pens and crayons for drawing or journalling
- copies of Ecclesiastes 3:1–8 for everyone
- CD player with appropriate background music
- bell to ring when shifting from writing to meditation
- worship centre set up to reflect the four directions of a Native medicine wheel: candle to symbolize the east, bowl of earth for the south, bowl of water for the west, incense, piece of driftwood, or barren branch for the north

Scripture

Ecclesiastes 3:1–8, Psalm 1, Revelation 22:1–2

Ecclesiastes 3:1–8 honours the seasons of life. Joan Chittester's *There Is a Season*[8] is a particularly good resource for those considering the levels of meaning of the times and seasons. The exquisite photos of John August Swanson's art would enhance any worship centre using this theme. You might also choose a scripture with an image of the tree of life, such as Psalm 1 or Revelation 22:1–2.

Reflection

The metaphor of the seasons of life has become a particularly powerful one for me. The Native medicine wheel integrates the wisdom of seasons of life and the powerful cycle of life through which we are always moving (see Gathering below).

We are constantly in a process of transformation after dying to one way, embracing the next stage. The medicine wheel gives a powerful lens through which we pay attention to this flow of life as one moves through the four directions, the four seasons, the four ages and stages of life and work. In some traditions, there are six directions, the other two being the sky and the earth.

For me the medicine wheel resonates powerfully with the times and seasons passage from Ecclesiastes. The path to spiritual maturity integrates all of the times and seasons of our lives and the movements of our souls.

Gathering **(Choose a, b, or c)**

a) If you were a tree, which season would you prefer?

b) If you are using the Ecclesiastes scripture, you might invite people in small groups to read the passage and respond to a season to which they are particularly drawn.

c) If your worship centre is set up to reflect the four directions, invite group members to reflect on where they find themselves in the circle. Read the following reflection, then share responses.

The east, where the sun rises, helps us to remember beginnings, such as spring, dawn, awakening, the coming of light into darkness. Reflect on what is beginning in your life. What is just beginning to come to light?

The south is where the sun is at its highest point. It is the direction from which warm winds blow, as in the heat of the summer. South is the spirit of earth, the power of life. It can represent the season of our life when we are hard at work in the outer world, working at our fullest. Reflect on what is in full bloom in your life; on where your energy is at its fullest point.

The west is the direction from which darkness comes. It brings the season of autumn, or the time of day when we rest and reflect. This is a season that honours the power of change, the place of dreams, of introspection, and of the unknown. This direction signifies purity and strength. Reflect on how this season connects with your life.

The north is the direction of the spirit of wind. The cold wind blows from the north as it cleanses and tests. It is the power of wisdom. Here we take time to reflect on what we began in the east, in the morning, in our youth, and on what has happened in all the seasons of our lives.

We give thanks for the great cleansing, testing wind that cuts through illusion. We honour the fallow times of our lives trusting that God will reveal the seeds that lie under winter snows awaiting a new beginning in the spring. We pray for the wisdom of experience. How does this season speak to your life?

Meditation

Close your eyes ... Become aware of this body-self that is you, as you come to meditation today ... Focus on your breath ... Notice the pattern of your breathing ... as it moves in ... as it moves out ... Follow your breath in ... Follow your breath out ... Notice how fast you are breathing ... Notice whether you are breathing deeply or with shallow breaths ... Notice where your body moves when you breathe ... Is the movement in your chest ... or in your belly? ...

Watch your breathing for a few minutes ... notice any changes that occur ... You may find that just attending to your breath will allow you to relax ... As you focus and breathe, let your breaths become slower and deeper ... Let your body relax and move to a place of peace ...

If you notice places where your body is sore or tense ... Imagine the breath moving to that place ... and gently massaging the tightened knots of tension ... or fear ... or anger ... or stress ... Simply allow the breath to open up your body ... so that your life energy can flow freely ... You are preparing yourself for prayer.

As you focus on your breathing ... you may notice thoughts coming and going ... Just notice the thoughts ... then let them go ... You may want to imagine them as clouds floating across the horizon ... or as leaves on a stream being carried away ... As thoughts arise ... gently return your focus to your breath ... Notice the space that opens inside you as you relax ... as you gradually come into your sacred centre ...

Ask God to bless this meditation journey and to use it for your highest good of mind ... body ... and spirit ...

I invite you to imagine yourself as a tree with leaves ... Allow the image of yourself as a tree to emerge ... What kind of tree are you? ... How large are you? ... Do you have any fruit or flowers? ... Get in touch with the texture of your trunk ... with the colour and smell of the tree that you are ... Are there any birds or small animals that find their home in you? ... Do children find you a place for shade and for playing and climbing? ...

Where are you planted? ... Are you alone ... or are there other trees nearby? ... Is the soil where your roots are planted well nourished ... or does it need care? ...

Notice your roots as they move deep into the earth ... Feel them as they reach out for what they need ... as they find their way around obstacles in the soil ... as they move deeply into the earth to draw up the nurture that you need from the earth ... Let the energy that comes from the earth move into your body ... as you allow it to rise in your trunk ... and flow into the branches and leaves ... Feel the energy of the sun ... of the air ... of the rain ... of the cosmos ... come into your being as it comes through your branches and leaves ... Know that you are deeply connected to the earth ... and to the sky ...

Feel the flow of that connection in your body ... Simply be the tree ... and listen for any wisdom the Spirit might have for your life as you experience yourself as this tree ...

Now imagine this tree as it goes through the cycles of the seasons ...

Imagine this tree in springtime ... Feel the warm sun on your branches and trunk and on the soil in which you are planted ... Feel it begin to awaken the flow of sap in you ... calling you to renew life once more ... Feel the beginnings of new buds in your branches that have withstood the harsh winter cold ... Feel the dormant energy in you begin to flow and awaken as the sun calls forth these buds ... as the sap nourishes the growth ... Feel the spring rains wash and nourish you ... Watch and imagine the leaves as they begin to form and the tree begins to blossom ... Feel the hope that awakens in this season ... the beginnings that are possible ... Notice how you feel about being this tree in this season ...

Now imagine the tree as it moves into summer ... Feel the fullness of your growth ... Feel the fiery summer sun beating down.... Imagine all the animals and birds that come for your shelter and nurturing ... Notice the shade you provide ... Feel any fruit that has come to fullness ... Notice the strength that it takes to withstand this fiery season ... the energy required for the growth ... Notice how you feel about being this tree in this season ...

Then notice the air as it begins to get cooler ... the light as it begins to fade ... the leaves as they begin to turn colour ... Notice the deepening colours of autumn ... the darkening skies ... Feel your leaves gradually dying ... gradually letting go and falling to earth ... Feel the autumn winds ... as they begin to blow away the leaves that are dying ... Notice the flow of sap in your branches slowing down ... preparing for a time of slowing down ... a time of inaction ... Notice how you feel about being this tree in this season ...

Feel the temperature getting colder as you move into the winter season ... Notice the north winds that test your integrity ... the snow that blankets you ... the barrenness of your branches ... Are there berries that remain in your branches that continue to nourish birds during this season? ... Feel the mystery of this season ... the silence of this season ... waiting in darkness with the sleeping earth ... all the while knowing that you hold dormant within you the seeds of new growth ... Notice how you feel about being the tree in this season ...

Then feel again the warming sun that begins to melt the ice in your branches ... that begins to take the snow from the earth ... whose waters nurture your roots ... Feel the lengthening of the days as the light returns ... Feel the stirring of new life within you called forth by the sun ... called forth by the awakening earth ... called forth by the Spirit of your Creator ...

Take some time to reflect on these seasons of the soul ... Take some time to notice how they speak to your life right now ... Be with the creating, gardening God ... and allow God to offer you the gift or wisdom the Creator would give you ...

Gradually and gently draw yourself back into this body-self that is you today ... Notice the breath again ... take some deep breaths as you reconnect with your body ... Make some gentle movements with your toes ... your fingers ... your head ... When you are ready, open your eyes.

Silence

Provide a time for journalling or drawing for those in the group who find this helpful.

Ring the bell at the end of the silent time to call people into the group again.

Debriefing

Invite participants to share what happened for them in this meditation.

Closure

a) Create your own "For everything there is a season" scripture:
- Have copies of the original scripture.
- Ask members to form pairs or groups of three and to write their own "For everything there is a season."

It is a powerful experience when people realize that scripture is not a dead thing and that we can rewrite the words for our times.

(I have led this exercise in many retreats but one of my favourite occasions was a women's retreat in Tatamagouche Retreat Centre in 2004: "A time to be imperfect and another time to be imperfect"!)

b) How was God with us today?

People call out a verb or phrase to the centre of the circle, which the leader can gather in closing prayer.

Prayer

God of the seasons and cycles of our lives.
We thank you for the wisdom of the turnings of our lives.
We thank you for your presence in all our times and seasons.
Help us to be present to the sacred rhythms of our lives.
Amen.

Meditation

5

The Communion of Saints

A Meditation for Gathering Strength of Spirit from Those Who Share Our Journey, Including Those Who Have Gone Before

Introduction

This meditation is useful for those who are grieving. It is also useful preparation for someone who has to do something she or he fears.

Preparation

- paper and pens for journalling
- CD player with appropriate background music
- bell to ring when shifting from writing to meditation
- worship centre with cloth, candle, open Bible, and photos of saints (They may be traditional saints from icons or photos, but remember to include pictures of modern "saints," people whose spirits embody the gospel values you cherish, such as Archbishop Desmond Tutu, Dorothy Day, Ghandi, Archbishop Oscar Romero, Mother Teresa, Karen Ridd, Rigobertu Mencha, Martin Luther King. You might also put in some unexpected saints, for example, photos of folks in the congregation or community who particularly reflect the presence of the Spirit.)
- tapers, metal flower box, or other metal container with sand or kitty litter (You may wish to invite participants to place tapers lit from the Christ candle in memory of those who have gone before. They can place the lighted candles in the metal container as part of the remembering ritual.)

Scripture

Romans 8:18-28, Ephesians 3:16-21

Either of these scriptures could work, depending on your group and its issues: Romans 8:18–28 speaks of creation groaning to birth freedom and wholeness for God's people. It also speaks of how the Spirit prays through us with sighs too deep for words. Ephesians 3:16–21 is a powerful prayer of empowerment. It speaks of God's Spirit inviting us to strengthen our inner being with power, of being rooted and grounded in love, and of knowing the love of Christ that surpasses knowledge so that we may be filled with all the fullness of God.

Reflection

When I was a "sophisticated," rational Christian, I found the image of the communion of saints to be irrelevant and archaic. After working as a pastor for many years, sitting at the bedsides of the dying, walking with the grieving, I have come to accept, almost in a literal way, the imagery and symbolism of the communion of saints. For I have indeed been "visited" by the spirit of those who have died, and felt the presence and energy of those who have gone before.

In worshipping with Latin American communities, I have experienced the naming of martyrs, including those who have disappeared in violent oppression. Each time a name is read, the congregation cries out "*Presente!*" meaning "Present!" Here, I am not dead. My spirit is still with you.

Westerners have a strong sense of individualism, but there is not one of us who has not built on the spirit, wisdom, and accumulated "knowing" of those who have gone before. We are all the beneficiaries of millions of years of evolution and thousands of years of spiritual experience.

The following meditation can be very useful for people needing to call on the strength and wisdom of others. It is powerful for times when someone has to do something that is daunting. I have used it to prepare women to go to court for custody issues or to confront an abuser. There are many other situations when we are afraid and need to call in the spirits and presence of our "communion of saints."

An alternative use of this meditation is to help people grieve and remember those loved ones who have died. Healthy grief used to be seen in terms of a person's ability to move on and let go. Those who have lost a loved one have told me that it is often difficult for them to find a place where they can talk about their loved one once a few months have passed after the death. They are told that they should be "over it" or that they should not "dwell in the past."

Increasingly, there is a recognition that although the person has died, the relationship continues, but in a different way. Healthy grieving is an ability to integrate the meaning and presence of the one who has died in such a way that it honours relationship, allowing the mourner to move forward. This takes time. It takes as long as it takes. Often the second year of grief is the hardest, for it is then that the reality of the loss begins to sink in.

Rituals around remembering and honouring are an important way for us to integrate the meaning of the person who has died into our ongoing life. They honour the memory and the person who is grieving. In some cases, these rituals help the person grieving to accept the reality of the loss.

Every All Saints' Sunday I lead a candle-lighting ritual in the congregation, naming people who have died in the past year. Family members light a candle in memory of them and place their candles in a metal window box in front of the communion table. Anyone in the congregation is invited to come forward to light a candle of remembrance. A prayer gathers these memories as we celebrate the light of the saints who are present with us in a communion of spirit.

Meditation

Close your eyes ... Let yourself pay attention to what it feels like to be in this body-self that is you right now ... Most of us go through whole days, sometimes our whole lives, without really paying attention to this body-self ... In Hebrew (the language system Jesus knew), there was no such thing as disembodied spirit ... They spoke of the *nephesh* ... the body soul ... the spirit body ... Jesus talked about our bodies as temples of the Spirit ... What is it like for you to think of yourself in that way? ...

As you begin to pay attention to your body ... do you notice places where tension is stored up ... places where your muscles are in tight knots? ... As you scan your body, from the top of your head to the bottom of your feet ... notice if there are tender places ... sore spots ... Send compassion to these places in your body... thank them for the hard work they are doing ... perhaps offer to pay more attention to what they are telling you in the future ... Continue to bathe the pain in your body with compassion and accepting love ...

Become aware of your breathing ... Our breath connects us with all that has been here since the beginning of creation ... Breathing ... this life-giving process goes on all of the time, even when we are unaware ... Notice if you are breathing with only a small part of your lungs ... or whether you are taking the breath deeply into your whole being ... Take the breath down to the bottom of your lungs ... up to the top of your shoulders ... Notice if your tummy moves in and out as you inhale and as you exhale ... the way a baby's does when breathing naturally, before its body has become tensed and locked up with the stress of living ...

Most of us breathe using only a limited lung capacity ... in bodies tightened up ... not fully open to the breath of life ... Let your body relax ... Let the tension flow out of your body through your feet ... Begin to allow your breath to move deeper into your being ... taking the breath into your heart, opening it up ... taking the breath deep down into your belly ... creating inner space ...

Breathe in deeply the healing presence of God ... the goodness and grace of God ... Take it right into the core of your being ... As you breathe out, let the breath carry with it the poisons—physical, emotional, and spiritual—that have built up in your system ... Breathe in the newness of possibility ... the hope that God gives ... Let go of the stress and tensions that are stored in your body-self ... in your emotional self ... in your spiritual self ... Breathe in life energy ... the creating breath of God that was there from the beginning ... Breathe out whatever would block you from being fully present to this time ...

Again notice your body ... If there are still tense places, imagine this healing breath moving directly to those spots ... loosening the tension ... letting go ... letting be ... letting open ... unlocking ... Notice the inner space that is being prepared and opened up inside you ... space for the sacred presence to find room ... space for the Holy One to be with you ... Your own sacred space ... your own holy ground ...

Imagine yourself in a safe and very sacred place for you ... It may be a place you know from your own history ... or it may be a place in your imagination ... Ground yourself in this place ... knowing that it is a place that God has given for the strengthening of your soul ... of your mind ... of your spirit ... Notice the colours and textures of this safe and sacred place ... Notice any odours, any images of what is around you ... Notice any feelings that arise as you are in this place ...

Once you feel fully present and grounded in this place ... call to your mind's eye those whom you know love and support you just as you are ... those whose love is unconditional ... They may be living ... they may be dead ... Call them to your mind's eye, one by one ... and invite them to offer you their words of wisdom or gifts of encouragement and strength ... If they were here with you right now ...

what would they say to you? ... What would they offer you? ... Allow each one in turn to pour out blessing ... wisdom ... strength ... encouragement to you ...

Let it flow over your body, surrounding you ...

Let it move into your whole being with love and empowerment ...

Feel their strength moving through you ...

Feel their wisdom moving through you ...

Feel yourself surrounded by this affirmation ... this deep connection with a cloud of witnesses ... a whole communion of those who love and support you ...

Know that you are not alone ...

(ALLOW A LONG SPACE FOR THIS TO HAPPEN.)

You may wish to call on others whose spirits you admire ... even if they do not personally know you ... You may wish to call on the presence of the courageous Mary ... the compassionate wisdom of Christ ... Sophia or one of the saints with whom you connect ...

Allow this sacred presence to pour out... blessing ... wisdom ... strength ... encouragement to you ...

Let it flow over your body surrounding you ...

Let it move into your whole being with love and empowerment ...

Feel the strength moving through you ...

Feel the wisdom moving through you ...

Feel yourself surrounded by affirmation ... this connection with a cloud of witnesses ... a whole communion of saints ...

Know that you are not alone ...

Invite the Spirit of Life to be with you ... to offer you the courage and the power that you need at this time ... Invite the Spirit to offer you any gift ... or wisdom that you might need for the struggle ... Allow yourself to receive this ...

Know that as you leave this meditative space ... you carry with you this communion of saints—this spiritual strength and support—as you move into your living ... You are not alone ... You live in God's world ... surrounded by God's presence ...

Gradually and gently draw yourself back to this place ... Notice again your breath as you breathe in ... as you breathe out ... Make some gentle movements with your toes and fingers ... some circles with your shoulders and head ... and as you feel ready ... open your eyes.

Silence

Provide a time for journalling and integrating the meditation. It may be helpful to write down any words or images of affirmation and encouragement you have received so that they may be handy for the times you might be tempted to forget.

Ring the bell at the end of the silent time to call people into the group again.

Debriefing

Share what happened for you in the meditation.

Closure

a) After sharing and writing down any insights people need to hang on to, have a box of tapers available and invite the participants to come forward to light a candle to honour and remember those who are part of their communion of saints. Invite them to share the wisdom or gift they have received from their saint or saints as they light the candle.

b) If you are using this meditation to prepare an individual going through a particularly difficult or frightening experience, take a stone, shell, or small container and pass it around the circle where each person symbolically fills it with the blessings and gifts of the communion of saints from the meditation, and the blessings and love of the community gathered. The person could carry this container with him or her into whatever frightening situation he or she must enter. It is a physical reminder of the communion of saints, and of the love and support the person carries with him or her.

c) Close with a gathering prayer or a time of silence to honour the Spirit.

Meditation

6

Journey up the Mountain on the Path to Wholeness

A Meditation for Those Who Are Ready for Deeper Spiritual Pilgrimage

Introduction

Preparation

- paper and pens for journalling
- worship centre with images of mountains from the Internet, or your own collection, such as Machu Picchu in Peru or other sacred places on mountains. The worship centre might also have a raised part in the middle with a candle on top
- loaf of bread and cup of wine to share as bread and blessing for the journey as part of the closure
- CD player with appropriate background music
- bell to ring when shifting from writing to meditation

Read carefully the scriptures suggested to determine which reading works best for your group.

Scripture

Exodus 19, Exodus 24:9–18, Exodus 33:12–23, Psalm 121, Mark 9:2–9

Scripture is full of stories of encounter with the Holy One on the mountaintop. One of the common names for God in Hebrew scripture is *El Shaddai*, sometimes translated as "God of the mountain" or "God of the breast." These scriptures speak of encounters on a mountaintop.

Reflection

In many cultures, those on a vision quest or spiritual pilgrimage go to high places. These places have often been experienced as "thin places," to use a term from the Celtic tradition. Here the veil between the sacred and the human condition seems very thin. The Holy and the human come close.

Travelling in England, Scotland, and Ireland one often sees ancient, hill-top stones and burial cairns that are witness to the sacred relationship of people in prehistoric times with high places. In Glastonbury,[9] a sacred path was built on a holy hill (called Glastonbury Tor) used by pilgrims for generations. Pilgrims still go on spiritual pilgrimages to high places like Tibet. Many mountain climbers or hikers speak of sacred experiences as they climb closer to the sky. They are able to capture a completely different perspective on the world and on their lives. A pilgrimage to a high place has become for many a metaphor of spiritual pilgrimage and awakening enlightenment.

Many scriptures refer to mountains as places of spiritual awakening.

If you are using this meditation while searching for community identity in times of transition, you may want to use one of the scriptures from Exodus. The mountain is the place where Moses and the Holy One (the One who has led them out of slavery) encounter one another, struggle with one another, and make a covenant relationship.

During the Exodus from Egypt, when the people find themselves in the wilderness, in a time of confusion and uncertainty, Moses goes up a holy mountain to meet God. (Exodus 19, then Exodus 24:9–18) He receives what the people at that time so desperately needed—a new covenant. This covenant gave boundaries and structures that Jewish people call "the Way" or the 10 words of God. In the Western church, we have traditionally and unimaginatively called these structures the Ten Commandments.

In the story, Moses keeps returning up the mountain because the people have such a hard time accepting this covenant that God has given them. Covenant living does not come naturally to most of us. It requires struggle to become attuned to a spirit path for our own lives and even more for the lives of whole communities.

There is a lovely part of the story in Exodus 33:12–23 where Moses is arguing with God about the relationship with the people and he actually changes God's mind. But Moses is only allowed to see the "back" side of God. This holy encounter leaves Moses radiant.

Psalm 121 uses the powerful imagery of looking to the hills for strength. Choose this scripture when members of the group need strength and support.

Mark 9:2–9 is the story of the transfiguration of Jesus, which also occurs on a high mountain and is reminiscent of Moses' encounter on the mountain. Jesus takes Peter, James, and John with him up a high mountain. There they have a powerful, sacred encounter that links them with the core traditions of their roots. They are also reminded of the baptismal promise that Jesus was God's beloved.

This story has been told for many historical reasons in tradition, but for meditation it can be used as a reminder of sacred encounter in thin places, where one is open to the living God's presence.

Gathering

a) Invite participants to share any experiences of walking or climbing in mountains.

b) Share the scripture that you have chosen (the direction that best suits your group). Share whatever parts of the Reflection work for your group.

Meditation

Close your eyes ... Become aware of this body-self that is you, as you come to meditation today ... Focus on your breath ... Notice the pattern of your breathing ... as it moves in ... as it moves out ... Notice how fast you are breathing ... Notice whether you are breathing deeply or with shallow breaths ... Notice where your body moves when you breathe ... Is the movement in your chest ... or in your belly? ...

Watch your breathing for a few minutes and notice any changes that occur ... You may find that just attending to your breath will allow you to relax ... As you focus and breathe ... let your breaths become slower ... and deeper ... Let your body relax ... and move to a sense of peace ...

Notice where your body is sore or tense ... Imagine the breath moving to that place and gently massaging the tightened knots of tension ... or fear ... or anger ... Simply allow the breath to open up your body ... so that your life energy can flow freely ... You are preparing yourself for prayer ...

As you focus on your breathing ... you may notice thoughts coming and going ... Just notice the thoughts ... then let them go ... You may want to imagine them as clouds floating across the horizon ... or as leaves on a stream being carried away ... Just as your lungs generate breath ... your mind generates thoughts ... As thoughts arise ... gently return your focus to your breath ... Notice the space that opens inside you as you relax ... as you gradually come into your sacred centre ...

Ask God to bless this meditation journey ... and to use it for your highest good of mind ... body ... and spirit ...

In your mind's eye ... imagine that you are feeling called to begin a sacred walking journey ... a pilgrimage that will take you closer to the Holy One ... Feel the desire rise up in you ... as you feel the invitation to the journey ... Feel the longing to draw closer to your Creator ... Let it rise up in you as you feel the invitation to the journey ...

Notice whether you begin your journey during the day or at night ... Notice if there is anyone coming on the journey with you ... The road is wide as you begin ... Notice your surroundings ... the colours ... the sounds ... the smells of the place where you begin your journey ... Notice if there are others with you on the path ... If there are ... choose how you will be with them ... in solitude or in companionship ... Notice what you are carrying with you as you begin this journey ... how you are prepared to take this pilgrimage ...

Imagine yourself walking along ... paying attention to the changes in environment around you as you journey ... At first, it is easy to walk ... but after a few hours you become fatigued ... and hungry ... and thirsty ...

Ahead you notice a small hut with a spring outside it ... and a cup inviting you to drink ... A wise person lives in this hut and invites you to come in to share food and drink and to rest ... and to talk about this journey ... You are welcomed warmly ... and listened to intently ... as you speak about why it is that you have begun this journey ... The wise person ... after hearing your story ... tells you that to go on ... you will have to look at what you must leave behind ...

"The path ahead is more demanding" ... you are told ... "You are entering a whole new level of journey ... This path leads to the top of the mountain ... where you will meet the sacred ... In order to go further ... you need to ask the Spirit what it is that you must leave behind so that you can move further on your path ... You may spend the night here in prayer, listening to the Spirit ... You may also decide that you are not ready to move forward ... and you may go back to where you began ... and respond to the invitation another time ... for the invitation will always be there."

As you spend time in this hut ... you become aware of the Spirit leading you to choose ... Notice the pull in opposite directions ... Notice what it is you must let go of in order to move forward ... Is this something you are ready and able to do? ...

If your choice is to move forward ... and you are able to let go of what holds you back ... prepare to join the journey again ... If you choose to go backward ... know that you can make that choice ... and leave this meditation now ... and that the invitation will come again ... perhaps at a time when you are more ready ...

As day breaks ... you share nurture for your body with the wise one ... You tell him or her what your decision has been ... and listen to his or her insights ...

If you move on with the journey ... the wise one offers you food and drink for the day ... and tells you that you will meet another rest place further up the mountain ...

The road becomes narrower today ... It begins to climb up a hill ... There are fewer people on this part of the journey ... At first, there are trees and lots of vegetation ... Gradually the path becomes narrower ... and the vegetation thins out ...

While walking, you realize how grateful you are that you are not carrying extra baggage at this point ... From time to time, you stop to rest ... and eat with gratitude the gift of food the wise one gave you ... As you eat and drink the water drawn from the spring ... you are aware of deepening insight and intention coming into your being ... You begin to notice the terrain with more intense awareness ... You can look out and see the path that you walked the day before ... and the many who walk it but do not choose the path up the mountain ... You can see ahead ... and the long journey that is still ahead ... It feels overwhelming ... but you have chosen the path to the Sacred ... and so you continue ... Each step becomes an intention to move forward ... Each step becomes a choice to release what would hold you back ... Your conscious awareness of what is happening inside your mind ... your body ... and your spirit seems to deepen with each step ... Your conscious awareness of the life around you also seems to deepen with each step ...

Just when you have run out of the food and water that you have been given ... and when you feel you have no more energy to continue forward ... you come to another small hut with a spring of water bubbling up just beside it ...

Another wise person greets and welcomes you warmly ... Again you are given what you need ... food and water for the body ... a warm welcome for the soul ... and an encouraging ... listening ... wise person who hears the story of your journey to this point ... Again, you know that you have been listened to very deeply ... known to the core of your being ...

This wise person helps you understand your increasing level of awareness as an essential part of the journey to the holy ... This person affirms your courage and openness to go this far ... and asks you if you are ready to continue the next day ... or whether you need some time to rest ... before you take the last day's journey to the top of the mountain where you will encounter the Sacred Source ...

You ask what you must do to continue ... Do you have to let go of more? ... The wise person tells you that you will continue to let go of what you need to as you journey ... but this is not the focus of this part of the way ... The focus needs to be on opening yourself ... preparing yourself for holy encounter ... allowing the desire that you felt at the initial invitation to journey to become stronger and stronger ... "This is a time to deepen intention" you are told ... "to know that you have been known and invited by Spirit to a holy place."

After a time of rest ... the wise person invites you to sit at a table where there is a loaf of bread and a cup of wine ... The wise person breaks the bread and shares it with you ... offering you bread for your journey ... You are given the cup to drink as you are offered blessing for your journey ... Again you are given what you need for the day and told that you are not to worry ... Your journey is being taken care of ... You will have what you need ... Just keep daring to walk ...

This day the path is much narrower ... You have to climb over rocks ... sometimes you have to find the path again ... You feel the intention to move closer to God grow more strongly in you ... and though the path is hard ... you know that you will not turn back ... You are more and more aware of the Mystery that lies ahead ... and of your longing to be closer to that Mystery ...

As you walk along you can see for miles ... You can see the path you walked the first day ... the path you walked the second day ... and you can see other pilgrims on the path both ahead of you and behind you ... You know that this is a journey that others have made before ... and that others will make after you ...

As the sun sets, you find yourself making the final distance to the top of the mountain ... You have climbed as far as you need to go ...

The path leads to a small clearing where there is a pool of water ... Exhausted ... you sit on the grass ... beside the water ... eating your last bit of bread ... wondering what will happen now ...

Soon a person in flowing garment comes to welcome you ... to thank you for coming ... You are given food and drink ... and told ... "Tonight you may prepare in whatever way you need for your meeting with the Holy."

You are invited to bathe in the sacred pool ... and given a new robe to put on ... After you have bathed and eaten ... notice if there is anything you need to do before you meet the Holy the next morning ... Are there questions that you need to ask? ... Are there deep needs that you are in touch with that you need to bring? ... Are there gifts you feel you need to offer? ...

You spend the night in rest and in prayer ... The next morning you are taken by the person you met the night before on the last part of your journey ... Feel the expectation arise in you as you approach ...

You come to a clearing where you meet the Sacred Presence who has been longing for your arrival ...

What is this Presence like? ... Notice what happens in this encounter ... Are words exchanged? ... gestures? ... Do you bring your questions ... your needs? ... Simply be before the Sacred Presence ... and allow that encounter to unfold ...

(LEAVE A LONG SILENCE.)

The Holy One desires to give you something ... to offer you a gift ... or wisdom for your life ... What is it that you are given? ... Take the time you need to experience this holy encounter ... to listen for what the Spirit desires for you at this time of your life ...

When you feel ready ... prepare to leave this holy place ... and this Holy Presence ... Do that in the way that feels right for you and for the Spirit you have encountered ...

Go back to the pool beside which you spent your night in preparation ... Give yourself some time to integrate the experience you have just had ... and the gift you have been given by the Spirit ... Notice if anything has changed in your mind ... in your body ... in your spirit ... as a result of this encounter ...

When you feel ready ... begin your journey down the mountain ... This time as you meet pilgrims on the way up ... you are able to encourage them ... as you encounter their longing ... so similar to your own ...

As you come to the home of the wise person ... you pass knowing looks ... and you realize that this person too has been to that holy place many times ... They remind you that your job now is to share your experience ... and to live it in the world at the foot of the mountain ...

Part of you wants to stay up there on the mountain ... but you recognize also the calling to return ... the calling to keep the hope of the Spirit alive ... the calling to keep God's dream alive ... the calling to live a transformed life out of this experience ...

And so you move down the path ... much easier than you ascended it ... And as you pass the last wise person's home ... you offer thanks to this one who guided you and showed you the way ...

Once at the foot of the mountain ... notice how it feels to be grounded in this place again ... Know that all that you gained from the journey returns with you ... Know that you now have the gift of the Spirit ... and the gift of the journey permanently within you ... It is there for you any time you need it ... Know that you also have the calling of the Spirit with you ... the calling to live a transformed life back where you began ... Know that you can make this journey again ... as many times as you need ...

Gradually and gently come back into awareness of your body-self ... Notice the breath as it moves in and out of your body ... Notice the feeling of the soles of your feet as they touch the floor ... Make some gentle movements of your toes and fingers ... some circles of your head to ground yourself in your body ... and return to this circle ... As you are ready, open your eyes ...

Silence

Make sure you allow enough time for participants to integrate their experience by writing or drawing in their journals, or by simply sitting quietly with the experience.

Ring the bell at the end of the silent time to call people into the group again.

Debriefing

Invite participants to share what happened for them in the meditation.

As the leader, pay attention to the work of the Spirit and reflect it back to the person sharing with everyone. This helps to ground the experience so that it is owned in the conscious mind and does not disappear into a state of forgetfulness or spiritual dilettantism.

If people can allow themselves to receive a spiritual gift and to own it in their own lives, this can be a transforming experience.

Closure

Offer a gathering prayer that invites people to share the gifts they have received from the experience.

Break the bread and offer it to the group as bread for the journey. Pass the cup and offer it as blessing for the journey.

MEDITATION

7

The Water of Life

Introduction

Preparation

- paper and pens for journalling
- worship centre with candle, bowl of water, and images of rivers and lakes
- CD player and appropriate background music
- bell to ring when shifting from writing to meditation
- music, such as "The River Is Here"[10], "Spirit of Life" (*Voices United* #381), "Spirit Dancing on the Waters" (*Voices United* #388)

Scripture

Revelation 22:1–2 or any scripture that refers to the River Jordan

Reflection

Water and flowing rivers are often used as metaphors for life. Intuitively, we know that the nature of life and spirit are like the nature of water in its many forms. Sometimes our lives flow freely, other times a part of our lives gets stuck in a stagnant pool. Sometimes life is leaping suddenly from one level to another, like a series of waterfalls. Sometimes the flow of life builds up behind an emotional or physical dam that seems to block the flow. Sometimes we need to find our way around potential obstacles to regroup on the other side. The metaphor of life as a flowing river has endless nuances and possibilities.

In our time, where water is seen as a commodity to be bought and sold rather than as a sacred gift of the Creator, it is important for people of faith to reclaim the sacredness of water. Water is essential for our individual lives and for the life of this planet. So here is an opportunity to reflect on water and its interconnection with life.

Gathering (Choose a, b, or c)

a) Use the music suggestions in the Preparation section of this meditation or choose a piece of music that suggests the flow of water in a river.

b) Invite participants to reflect on their life as a river.
   - How is your river of life flowing right now?
   - What comes to mind as you think about your life as a river?

c) Read the scripture you have chosen. I particularly like the passage from Revelation as it connects with the rivers in the Genesis story of creation and speaks of the flow of the river of life right in the middle of the city, not only in the garden as in Genesis.

Meditation

Shut your eyes and let your body relax ... Let it sink into the chair or into the floor ... Let yourself be held up ... supported by the chair or floor ... You do not need to do the work of holding up your body ... You can let it be supported ... You can let go and relax ...

Begin to notice your breathing ... Breath is essential to living ... It was God's breath that we are told created all that is ... It has the power for cleansing and healing not only our physical system ... but also our emotional and spiritual lives ... Notice the breath as it begins at the tip of your nose ... Feel the cool air as it moves through your nostrils ... Follow it as it moves across the roof of your mouth ... Follow it as it goes down into your windpipe ... Follow it as it goes through your bronchial tubes into your lungs ... Notice where it goes in your lungs ... Notice how deeply the breath of life is moving within you ...

Gradually allow yourself to soften and flow with the breath ... Let your shoulders fall and relax as you breathe into the part of your lungs high up in you shoulders ... Let your tummy muscles relax as you let the breath move deeply into your whole torso ... Notice what it feels like to be in your body-self as this happens ... Notice the feeling of letting go ... of relaxing ... of well-being ... of inner space that is created ... Just be present to the breath as it moves in ... as it moves out ... in and out ... in and out ...

Notice the space that opens inside you as you relax ... as you gradually come into your sacred centre ...

Take a few moments to settle your mind ... Let your mind become still like a crystal mountain lake ... Let your breathing become like the gentle wind in the trees ... It rises and falls with no effort on your part ... Its whisper brings only peace ... Let your thoughts be like gentle ripples on the lake ... They are not important ... they cannot disturb the deep stillness below the surface ... As thoughts arise ... gently return your focus to your breath ...

Now imagine yourself as part of the water of a crystal mountain lake ... Notice the coolness of the water ... Notice the clarity of the water that has collected from mountain springs and falling rain ... It is as if you are just beginning ... fresh ... new ...

Then you feel yourself being drawn towards a particular part of the lake where there is movement ... Little by little, you move along until you find yourself part of a stream ... You sense yourself as part of something great ... moving along the face of the earth ... never quite knowing where you are going ... but always drawn ahead ... You are drawn by a force that is so much a part of your existence that you forget it is there ... It motivates every move you make ... but the force is invisible to you ... and as you grow and as its effect on you increases ... you become less and less aware of it ...

Then you find yourself part of a larger stream ... It grows and gains momentum ... Soon your stream is a river ...

Notice the river that you have become ... Notice what it feels like as your river carries you along more swiftly now ... Notice how the speed of your flow has increased ... but also how the turbulence and pace increases ... You find yourself swept along through dark canyons and down roaring rapids ...

Sometimes you come to a rock that blocks the way ... Notice how you are led to flow around it as you continue your journey ... Sometimes time seems to slow down as you hang almost suspended in stagnant pools ... held by the force ... but cut off from the flow ... Sometimes you find yourself at a point of major transformation ... where the level you have been flowing at drops in a waterfall ... Notice what it feels like to let go of the level you had been flowing at ... and to be carried to a new level of life-flow ... Notice the feeling of having survived the rushing waterfall and of arriving at the bottom of the falls in a pool that swirls around in circles until it is able to move forward ...

Somewhere along the way you may find yourself behind a great dam ... However it has gotten there, it slows your path ... and harnesses your power ... For a time the flow of the river is blocked ... You are confined ... and under pressure ... You may be trapped there for a long while ... But you keep remembering the rightness you felt in your free-flowing state higher on the mountain ... You do not forget what freedom feels like ... You keep longing for it ...

Eventually, you find yourself beyond the dam ... and again you feel the flow ... You are free to move forward ... to follow the force that draws you forward ... and perhaps because of this experience you are more aware of the importance of this spiritual force that draws you along your way ...

As you flow in your river ... you become aware of other life that depends on you ... Your river is full of plants and animals ... These life forms take you for granted because you are all they know ... You form the structure for their existence ... When you are healthy and clean ... life grows in you ... When you lose your healthy flow ... life dims and dies ... On your banks grow trees and shrubs and flowers nurtured by the water you bring ... Children come to play in you ... Animals come to drink from you ...

You begin to recognize that you have a profound connection with the land through which you flow ... the banks that hold you ... the stones that affect your course ... the bits of wood and leaf that are carried by your flow ...

You gain the wisdom of knowing that you are part of a flow of life ... that is greater than the river that you are ... You come to see how the flow of your water affects the life around you ... and how the flow of life around you affects you ...

What is beyond the banks that hold you in is a mystery ... but you know it is awesome and great ...

As your journey draws on ... you become aware that the banks that hold you in are no longer apparent ... You have become part of the great sea ... And you recognize that you are not at the end of the journey ... for the sea gives birth to wind and rain ... Rain gives life to land, and land carries the river back to the sea ... You know that you are connected profoundly to the flow of life ... in ways that you cannot understand ... and to the Source of that flow ...

Take some gentle time to allow these images to rest in your soul ... and listen for the wisdom that the Spirit of Life would give you about the flow of your life right now ...

Gradually and gently draw yourself back to this place ... making gentle circles with your head and shoulders ... gentle movements with your fingers and toes ... When you are ready ... open your eyes.

Silence

Allow time for journalling for those who wish.

Ring the bell at the end of the silent time to call people into the group again.

Debriefing

Share the wisdom that came for you in this meditation.

Closure

How has the Spirit been flowing among us this day (one word or phrase)?

Sing "Spirit of Life" (*Voices United* #381) or one of the other music suggestions at the beginning of this meditation.

Part III

Meditations for Slowing Down

MEDITATION

8

Being Present

A Waking Meditation

One of my favourite stories follows:

"Where shall I look for Enlightenment?" the disciple asked.

"Here," the elder said.

"When will it happen?" the disciple asked.

"It is happening right now," the elder answered.

"Then why don't I experience it?" the disciple persisted.

"Because you do not look," the elder said.

"But what should I look for?" the disciple continued.

"Nothing. Just look," the elder said.

"But at what?" the disciple asked again.

"At anything your eyes alight upon," the elder answered.

"But must I look in a special kind of way?" the disciple went on.

"No. The ordinary way will do," the elder said.

"But don't I always look the ordinary way?" the disciple said.

"No, you don't," the elder said.

"But why ever not?" the disciple asked.

"Because to look you must be here. You're mostly somewhere else," the elder said.[11]

Most of the time, we are somewhere else rather than being fully present in the moment we are living.

In Part I, Chapter 1, I wrote about one of the emotional, physical, and spiritual challenges of our time. Many of us are "tuned in" or "turned on" to a fast pace of life, lived as a response to external demands. This hyper vigilance becomes addictive, and it becomes very difficult to shift to "being time."

"Being time" is where we are in tune with the rhythms of our soul, of our feelings, of our internal world beyond the surface reality. "Being time" is essential for us to be able to be fully present to other persons, to the creation around us, and to ourselves and to God.

I am including a simple practice for people to use to begin to make this shift, which you can do as a waking meditation, on the bus, or while driving home from work. You can do it in the car just before going into your home or at any time when you start to recognize that you are becoming a "human doing" instead of a human being. Do it when you want to stop the merry-go-round and reconnect with yourself.

This kind of practice or the walking meditation that follows helps you to be more "awake" and more "alive" to what is going on around you. You will notice things that you might totally miss otherwise, such as the look in your child's eyes, the colour and scent of the garden, the life that is in you and in the world around you.

Meditation

Bring your attention to your body-self ... Chances are you have been living "outside" your body all day ... Try to notice the skin on the bottom of your feet ... Just bring awareness there ... Your feet ground you ... root you to the earth ... When we live in a fast-paced head space, we are no longer grounded ... Imagine that the bottom of your feet open to the earth so that you draw your energy and attention to your feet and become grounded ...

Begin to notice your breath ... Be aware of where in your body your breath is moving ... Notice how your breath begins to move more deeply as you pay attention to it ... Let each breath deepen your relaxation and help you to let go ... Imagine each breath out, carrying with it the stress and worries of the day ... They will be there tomorrow to pick up if necessary ...

Feel the tension flowing out of your shoulders as you do this ... Feel the tension flowing down your arms and out of your hands ... Feel the tension flowing down your back ... Feel it flowing down your back and out through your trunk ... and feel the tension flowing out of your stomach as your stomach lets go ... Feel the tension flowing down your legs and out of the bottoms of your feet ...

Bring your awareness to your heart ... Imagine the breath opening your heart ... allowing it to fill with feeling ... with love ...

If you are coming home to be with people ... be aware of people for whom you want to be fully present ... Open your heart space to them so that you can go to be fully with them ...

Ask the Spirit to keep you aware of the sacredness of your body ... of the sacredness of relationship ... of the sacredness of being with another ... and of being present to yourself ...

Take some time in silence simply "to be" ... and to notice what is happening inside you ....

MEDITATION

9

Opening to God in Creation

A Simple Walking Meditation

Introduction

This meditation can be done individually or in a group. Hopefully it can be done outdoors. But a walking meditation can be done anywhere. It is helpful to prepare for intentional "being" with God in creation. It would be good for a youth group, for worship at a summer camp, or as an activity at a retreat. It could even be used with an older children's program on a Sunday morning.

Preparation

Read the Reflection below so that you will be able to explain "walking meditation," using words that speak to the age level of those with whom you are working.

Choose one scripture reading as a focus. Following are some suggestions, but feel free to choose others that speak to you or to your group.

Scripture

Psalm 16:11, Psalm 25:5, Psalm 33:5, Psalm 36:9, Psalm 46:10, Psalm 104:24, Psalm 107:35, Psalm 139:13–14, John 10:10

Reflection

Many traditions use a simple meditative experience that involves walking and being intentionally present to the moment. Walking meditation involves mindful walking, bringing awareness to the feeling of the feet as they touch the earth or floor, being aware of the movement of the body as it walks. It is about being intentionally in the experience of the moment. Most of us spend the largest part of our lives distanced from the experience of being fully present—to ourselves, to our world, to the nudging of God's Spirit.

Walking meditation can be done anywhere: on the street, in the corridors where you work, in a park. It can also be done in labyrinths, which have become more commonly used in our congregations over the past 10 years. You might research labyrinths in a library or on the Web, for example, www.gracecathedral.org/labyrinth. Searching on the Internet brings rich reading about not only creating but also using labyrinths for walking meditation.

You can walk a question, a feeling, a struggle, a grief process, a scripture, or any kind of spiritual work. You can simply walk with an openness to listen for God and with a desire to be fully present in the moment.

If you do not have access to a labyrinth, a simple way to introduce people to walking meditation is to invite them to a time of mindful relaxation and silence.

I often use a simple line from a psalm or other scripture as a mantra to centre and focus. The line from scripture takes on new nuances and meanings as you walk intentionally with it. At times, one word may jump out more powerfully from the passage. Simply allow the experience to open you to the nudging of God's Spirit.

Gathering

Explain "walking meditation." Explain to the group participants where they are allowed to walk and when they should return.

Explain that you are going to lead a brief meditation and give them a line from scripture that you would like them to use for focus as they walk. Then they are free to get up and move in silence and to walk in silence until the time they are to return to the circle.

Invite group members to be still and centre themselves as they let themselves relax and experience being in their body. This should be done while they are seated.

Meditation

Close your eyes ... become aware of this body-self that is you, as you come to meditation today ... Focus on your breath ... Notice the pattern of your breathing ... as it moves in ... as it moves out ... Notice how fast you are breathing ... Notice whether you are breathing deeply or with shallow breaths ... Notice where your body moves when you breathe ... Is the movement in your chest or in your belly? ...

Watch your breathing for a few minutes and notice any changes that occur ... You may find that just attending to your breath will allow you to relax ... As you focus and breathe let your breaths become slower and deeper ... Let your body relax and move to a sense of peace ...

Notice where your body is sore or tense ... Imagine the breath moving to that place ... and gently massaging the tightened knots of tension ... or fear ... or anger ... Simply allow the breath to open up your body so that your life energy can flow freely ... You are preparing yourself for prayer ...

As you focus on your breathing ... you may notice thoughts coming and going ... Just notice the thoughts then let them go ... You may want to imagine them as clouds floating across the horizon or as leaves on a stream being carried away ... As thoughts arise, gently return your focus to your breath ... Notice the space that opens inside you as you relax ... as you gradually come into your sacred centre ...

Ask God to bless your walking meditation and to use it for your highest good of mind, body, and spirit ... As you walk, I invite you to allow the following scripture to resonate in your mind ... in your body ... in your spirit ... and in your experience.

(REPEAT SLOWLY THE SCRIPTURE YOU HAVE CHOSEN, THEN ALLOW THE GROUP TO GET UP AND MOVE.)

Part IV

Experiencing the Healing God through Scripture

MEDITATION

10

Coming Home

Introduction

Preparation

- pens and papers for journalling
- CD of soft background music
- bell to ring when shifting from writing to meditation
- worship centre with candle, open Bible, and photos or symbols of reconciliation and forgiveness

Scripture

Luke 15:11–32

Reflection

The story of the homecoming of the prodigal son is one of the parables that speaks most powerfully to the human condition. It is an archetypal story of being lost and being found, of sibling rivalry and parental love. It is really about God's unconditional acceptance and love and God's longing for reconciliation and relationship.

It is a powerful story because we can all find ourselves in one or more of the characters. This meditation invites us to identify with the lost son, the one who has lost his way. It is particularly helpful for those who are experiencing deep shame and feel that they can never be loved because of how they have behaved.

Our lives may or may not have led us into the risky behaviour of the younger son in the story. However, there is in all of us a part that feels lost and disconnected from what we know to be our true home.

Gathering

Lectio divina is a simple and powerful tool for listening for God through praying with scripture. It has long been used by the Jesuits and other contemplatives as a form of prayer. The North American Protestant tradition is rediscovering this spiritual practice through the Christian base communities in Latin America. Sometimes it has been called the African Bible Study since Western theologians discovered it being used in a missiological institute in South Africa.

For those unfamiliar with *lectio divina*, explain that it is about listening with the whole being for the way God would speak to us today through the scripture. It is a form of prayer. It is not an analytical discussion or Bible study.

Explain that Luke 15:11–32 will be read three times, each time with a different question. After each reading, there is silence, then people will be invited to offer any insight they have heard without discussion.

1) Invite people to notice a word, phrase, or image that stays with them as you read the passage.

   Read the passage through slowly.

   Allow a time of silence.

   Invite sharing.

2) Invite people to reflect on how this passage connects with something in their own life experience.

   Read the passage again (perhaps by someone of a different gender).

   Allow a time of silence.

   Invite sharing.

3) Invite people to listen for where God might be challenging them or our world with a word of life or growth through the passage.

Read the passage again (perhaps by a third voice).

Allow a time of silence.

Invite sharing.

You may choose to close with the Lord's Prayer.

Meditation

Close your eyes ... Notice what it feels like to be in this body-self that is you right now ... Most of us go through whole days, sometimes whole lives ... without paying attention to this body-self ... In Hebrew (the language system Jesus knew) there was no such thing as disembodied spirit ... they spoke of the *nephesh* ... the body soul ... the spirit body ... Jesus talked about our bodies as temples of the Spirit ... What is it like for you to think of yourself in that way? ...

As you begin to pay attention to your body ... do you notice places where tension is stored up ... places where your muscles are in tight knots? ... As you scan your body ... from the top of your head to the bottom of your feet ... notice if there are tender places ... and send compassion to these places in your body ... thanking them for the hard work they are doing ... You might offer to pay more attention to what they are telling you in the future ...

Become aware of your breathing ... this life-giving process that goes on all of the time ... even when we are not conscious of it ... Notice if you are breathing with only a small part of your lungs ... or whether you are taking the breath deeply into your whole being ... down to the bottom of your lungs ... up to the top of your shoulders ...

Notice if your tummy moves in and out as you inhale ... as you exhale ... This is how a baby breathes when it is breathing naturally ... before its body has become tense and locked up with the stress of living ... Open your body to the breath of life ... Let your body relax ... Let the tension flow out of your body through your feet ... Begin to allow your breath to move deeper into your being ...

Take the breath deep down into your belly ... Breathe in deeply the healing presence of God ... the goodness and grace of God ... Take it right into the core of your being ... As you breathe out ... let the breath carry with it the poisons ... physical ... emotional ... spiritual that have built up in your system ... Breathe in the newness of possibility ... Breathe in the hope that God gives ... Let go of the stress and tensions that are stored in your body-self ... in your emotional self ... in your spiritual self ... Breathe in life energy ... the creating breath of God that was there from the beginning ... Breathe out whatever would block you from being fully present to this time ...

Again notice your body ... If there are still tense places, imagine this healing breath moving directly to those spots ... loosening the tension ... letting go ... letting be ... letting open ... letting unlock ... Know that you are in a safe place ... Notice the inner space that is being prepared and opened up inside you ... space for the sacred presence to find room ... space for the Holy One to be with you ... your own sacred space ... your own holy ground ...

I invite you to imagine yourself as the young person in the story Jesus told ... You have left home ... You have turned away from everything that you had been raised to respect ... You have become lost to family ... to God ... to yourself ... You hardly know who you are any more ... so far from your centre you have come ...

Be in touch with the feeling of being lost ... of being separated from love ... separated from relationship ... living in a way that is self-betraying ...

Feel the desire rising up in you to return ... the longing to be back in a safe place ... In your mind's eye ... make the decision to go home ...

Imagine yourself on the road ... with your apologies ready ... with all of your excuses prepared ... afraid of the reaction you will get ... Will you be yelled at? ... embarrassed? ... told that you made your bed ... now you should lie in it? ... As you get nearer to home, feel the anxiety rise about whether you will be accepted ...

But then before you even get home ... someone is coming ... You lower your eyes ... not daring to look into the eyes and face of the other ... You begin to go down on your knees ...to say how sorry you are ...and how you wish you had not done what you had done ...

But even before you have had the chance to speak, you are lifted up ... Your face is taken in the other's hands ... You look into the eyes of the one who meets you ... and all you see is love ... and all you feel is welcoming embrace ... and tears of joy that you are safe and that you are home ... No questions ... no judgment ... no excuses ... only welcoming love ...

Allow yourself to rest in that embrace for as long as you are able ... Allow yourself to hear what is spoken into your ear ... Listen for what God would want to say to you at this time ...

Gradually and gently draw yourself out of this embrace ... knowing that those arms are there to hold you whenever you need to return to them ... Draw yourself from the meditation scene ... and gradually connect with this body-self that is you right now ... Make some gentle movements with your fingers and toes ... some movements with your neck ... Begin to notice your breath again ... this breath that has been breathing you all the time you have been meditating ... even if you have not paid attention to it ... As you are ready, open your eyes ...

Silence

Provide a time for journalling or drawing for those who find it helpful.

Ring the bell at the end of the silent time to call people into the group again.

Debriefing

a) Write the words that come to you as you remember and reflect on this meditation.

b) What was it like for you to be welcomed home? What did the Spirit want to say to you through this meditation?

MEDITATION

11

Calm in the Storm

Introduction

Preparation

- pens and papers for journalling
- CD of soft background music
- bell to ring when shifting from writing to meditation
- worship centre with candle, open Bible, photos or symbols of the sea, such as sea shells, driftwood, beach glass, model of a fishing boat, and of storms at sea

Scripture

Mark 4:35–41

Reflection

This experience happens in a time of crossing over, a time and place of transition. It happens in an evening time, as dark approaches. It happens after a day of profound teaching. Jesus had been sharing parables with those who came to learn from him, with those who wanted to experience this teacher of God. It happens in the extremity of fear and panic. It happens when the disciples are experiencing abandonment. They feel that Jesus does not even care about them.

These are seasons of the soul with which most people can identify. We have all been in places where we felt that the winds of change were going to overpower us, when we felt that we were going under, where we felt abandoned by God or by those close to us. We have also been in places where we needed another person to still us with assurance that we will be all right and that the storms of our lives will be stilled.

You may know as well that in Hebrew scripture the sea is a symbol of chaos. In creation, the Spirit breathed over the seas of chaos and brought order and created dry land.

Gathering (Choose a or b)

a) Read Mark 4:35–41 slowly and with expression.

   You could do this using the *lectio divina* model outlined in the previous meditation (see page 90).

b) Questions for sharing:
   - When have you found yourself in a place of transition, in a place of crossing over, in a place where one time is ending and another not yet begun?
   - Have you ever had a time when
     - you felt that you were going under?
     - it felt as if the storm around you was going to swallow you up?
     - the winds of change blew so strongly that you almost capsized?
   - Have you ever had an experience of one who said, "Peace, be still!" in such a way that it had the power and authority to calm the storm you were going through?

Meditation

Close your eyes ... Become aware of this body-self that is you, as you come to meditation today ... Focus on your breath ... Notice the pattern of your breathing ... as it moves in ... as it moves out ... Follow your breath in ... Follow your breath out ... Notice how fast you are breathing ... Notice whether you are breathing deeply or with shallow breaths ... Notice where your body moves when you breathe ... Is the movement in your chest ... or in your belly? ...

Watch your breathing for a few minutes ... notice any changes that occur ... You may find that just attending to your breath will allow you to relax ... As you focus and breathe, let your breaths become slower and deeper ... Let your body relax and move to a place of peace ...

Notice where your body is sore or tense ... Imagine the breath moving to that place ... and gently massaging the tightened knots of tension ... or fear ... or anger ... or stress ... Simply allow the breath to open up your body ... so that your life energy can flow freely ... You are preparing yourself for prayer.

As you focus on your breathing ... you may notice thoughts coming and going ... Just notice the thoughts ... then let them go ... You may want to imagine them as clouds floating across the horizon ... or as leaves on a stream being carried away ... As thoughts arise ... gently return your focus to your breath ... Notice the space that opens inside you as you relax ... as you gradually come into your sacred centre ...

Ask God to bless this meditation journey for you to use it for your highest good of mind ... body ... and spirit ...

In that place, I invite you to imagine yourself beside a large lake or sea ... standing on the shore ... Notice the smell of the sea ... the colours of the water ... of the sky ... of the boats ... Notice the sun beginning to set in the west and the sense that you need to leave this place in order to cross over to the other side ... Your time on this side is over ...

Allow yourself to feel the call to be in another place ... the invitation to leave one way of being ... to let go ... and to enter a journey of transition ... Notice if the Spirit wants to offer you that invitation for your own life ...

Imagine getting into a small boat with Christ, who will make this journey with you ... indeed, who has invited you on this journey ... As you move out to the middle of the lake ... you notice that Christ has fallen asleep ... exhausted after a hard day ... The boat's rocking motion is soothing in a calm sea ... The sunset deepens and sinks behind the horizon ... and darkness begins to fall ...

Suddenly there is a large wind that is very frightening ... a storm seems to come when you least expect it ... There is chaos ... Life is turned upside down ... You feel as if you might go under ... It is a frightening time ... and you begin to wonder where Christ is ... You feel abandoned by Christ ... You begin to feel Christ does not even care about the danger you are in ... Angrily you cry out to Christ to wake up ... to pay attention to your needs ...

Christ looks with deep compassion at you ... recognizes your panic ... and speaks to the storm ... and to you ... saying ... "Peace ... be still ... Peace ... be still ... Peace ... be still" ... and the storm begins to subside ... and the winds that threaten become calm ... and the waves that seemed to engulf you become still ... and the chaos inside you becomes more tranquil ... The fear subsides ... The angry blaming calms down ... Your anxiety is replaced by a sense of deep peace ... of being centred ... You can breathe again ... You are coming home to a deep knowing ... that you are not alone ... You live in God's world ... and you know that you are connected with the Source of all that is ...

Let the Christ speak to the storms and chaos that are part of your life ... "Peace ... be still ... Peace ... be still ... Peace ... be still ..."

Is there any other message the Spirit would like to speak into your places of transition ... your places of chaos and fear? ...

(LEAVE A LONG SILENCE.)

Gradually and gently draw yourself from this place ... knowing that you can return here whenever you wish ... Draw yourself from the meditation scene ... and gradually connect with this body-self that is you right now ... Make some gentle movements with your fingers and toes ... some movements with your neck ... Begin to notice your breath ... again this breath that has been breathing all the time you have been meditating ... even if you have not paid attention to it ... As you are ready ... open your eyes.

Silence

Provide a time for journalling or drawing for those who find it helpful.

Ring the bell at the end of the silent time to call people into the group again.

Debriefing

a) If they have not already been doing it during the silence, invite people to write or draw in their journals about what they experienced in the meditation. Make sure you leave enough time for journalling, as it helps to ground the meditation.

b) The second stage of grounding the meditation experience is to invite people to share their experience in their own way.

Closure

Invite the group members to offer one word or phrase about how they have experienced God being with them in this time. Gather these in simple prayer.

MEDITATION

12

Allowing God to Speak to Our Place of Exile

Introduction

This meditation is particularly effective for those experiencing alienation.

Preparation

- paper and pens for journalling
- CD player with appropriate background music
- bell to ring when shifting from writing to meditation
- worship centre that includes symbols of desert or exile, lonely faces, wilderness

Scripture

Isaiah 35:1–6, as well as other passages from Isaiah

Reflection

Many theologians in our time have adopted the metaphor of exile to speak of the state of the modern church. Walter Brueggemann is the master of exile theology and has helped the modern church find a language for our experience. (See Bibliography, page 179, for books written by Walter Brueggemann.)

Like those carried off into Babylon in the sixth century BCE, this generation has to deal with the ending of an era, an ending of "the way things have been." The God who blesses political power, for the most part, belongs to the past. Religion, linked with political power, which we have known as Christendom, is indeed dead (even if it still breathes its last gasps of life in the U.S.A. today). Often today the church has difficulty being heard in places of power, especially since we often come to these places as critics of social policies that marginalize the poor or of political decisions that support powerful interests and harm creation.

Exile is a place where one way of being has ended and another has not yet begun. Exile is "between time," between the time when we knew the questions and some of the answers, and the time when we are forced to ask new questions that we have not yet been able to formulate. Exile happens as paradigms shift and we do not feel at home in the radically rearranging world.

But exile is also profoundly personal. When we are given a diagnosis of terminal illness, we are thrown into exile. When our partner leaves us, we are thrown into exile. When the job we thought would always give us security is suddenly wrenched from us, we are thrown into exile.

Some exiles we choose. We enter them because we know we need to radically reorient our lives. Other exiles are forced upon us, and we are dragged into them kicking and screaming. Either way, exile is a time of grieving for what has been lost, of living with uncertain transition, of figuring out who we are in this new reality into which we have been thrust. Eventually exile is also about allowing the "new thing God is doing" to emerge even when it is not very clear at the time.

The biblical exile was traumatic. It etched its pain and story into the soul of Judaism. But it was also a time when people returned to their stories and found deep meaning in them. It was a time when scripture was collected and written down. (The first creation story in Genesis comes from this experience.) It was a time for prophets called forth by the Spirit. And it was a time when a whole new way of being a people of God emerged. The synagogue movement, a lay movement away from the temple priestly tradition, emerged out of necessity from this period of being cut off from the temple and institutional religion.

So exile, when one can look back on it with 20/20 vision, is, indeed, a time of transformation.

Gathering

a) Have you ever felt like a stranger in a strange land, a long way from home? What was that like for you?

b) Have you ever had someone speak to you in a way that woke you up to your potential or possibility in your life? What was that like for you?

Meditation

This meditation is in two parts. The first part invites us into the experience of the exiles in Babylon. After this, the scripture is spoken into that experience while the group remains still in sacred space. Following that, the group is invited to experience a more personal reflection on the images of the scripture. This meditation works best when led slowly with lots of space for silence.

Close your eyes ... Focus on your breathing ... Notice the pattern of your breathing ... How fast are you breathing? ... Would you say your breath is fast or slow ... shallow or deep? ... Where does your body move when you breathe? ... Is the movement in your chest ... or in your belly? ...

Watch your breathing for a few minutes ... and notice any changes that occur ... You may find that just attending to your breath will allow you to relax ... As you focus and breathe ... let your breaths become slower and slower ... deeper and deeper ... Let your body relax and move to a sense of peace ...

As you focus on your breathing ... you may notice thoughts coming and going ... Just notice the thoughts and then let them go ... Just as your lungs generate breath ... your mind generates thoughts ... As thoughts arise ... return your focus to your breath ... Notice the space that opens inside you as you relax ... as you gradually come into your sacred centre ...

Ask God to bless this meditation journey ... and to use it for your highest good of mind ... of body, and ... of spirit ...

In your imagination ... I invite you to enter into the experience of the Hebrew people to whom this word is addressed ... They had been defeated ... overcome by the conquering Babylonian empire ... Jerusalem was destroyed ... Many had died in the siege ... and many more had died when the victors marched the leaders of Judah into exile in Babylon across a barren desert ...

In Babylon, the Hebrew people were not in a lot of physical danger ... but they were not at home ... They were in a place where they did not have free choice to leave ... a place where they did not have roots ... a place where their culture and faith were mocked ... They were in a place where they were not even certain who had survived back in Judah and what was happening there ...

In your imagination, enter Babylon as one of the exiles ... Feel the heat of the place ... the desert sun ... the sand in the air when the wind blows ... Feel the foreignness of the place ... the sense that you do not belong here ... You are a stranger in a strange land ...

Feel the sense that there is nothing you can do to change the situation ...

Your institutions are not allowed ... It is difficult to meet with others who have had the same experience as you ...You feel isolated ...

You have enough to eat ... You are not a slave ... but you are not free either ... and your soul is starving for the stories of your people ... for the stories of your God ... for stories of home ... and how it used to be when God was with you ... Now it seems as if God has forgotten you ... Feel your longing for roots ...

And then come these words of a prophet from home ... a man named Isaiah ... who kindles life in your heart ...

(READ ISAIAH 35:1-6 VERY SLOWLY.)

"The wilderness and the dry land shall be glad, the desert shall rejoice and blossom; like the crocus it shall blossom abundantly, and rejoice with joy and singing. The glory of Lebanon shall be given to it, the majesty of Carmel and Sharon. They shall see the glory of the LORD, the majesty of our God. Strengthen the weak hands, and make firm the feeble knees. Say to those who are of a fearful heart, 'Be strong, do not fear! Here is your God. God will come with vengeance, with terrible recompense. God will come and save you.'

"Then the eyes of the blind shall be opened, and the ears of the deaf unstopped; then the lame shall leap like a deer, and the tongue of the speechless sing for joy. For waters shall break forth in the wilderness, and streams in the desert."

Notice how these words make you feel ...

Be in touch with a time when you felt in exile as did the Israelites, to whom these words were spoken ... Pay attention ... as you are able ... to all of the feelings associated with that experience ... with that time in your life ... If you were to think of desert times ... of the wilderness times of your own life ... what would they be? ...

Isaiah promised streams of living water in the desert that would heal the land ... and cause flowers to grow where before there had only been desolation ...

Can you remember a time in your own life when new life blossomed in unexpected places? ... How did that happen for you? ... What did it feel like when the beginnings of hope and promise began to stir in you? ... When hope became awakened ... just when you had all but given up? ...

What helped you move out of your wilderness time (if you did)? ... What did you need to hear at that time? ... Did this happen for you ... or not? ...

How was God for you in that time? ...

Isaiah promised healing of seeing ... of hearing ... of unbinding those who were lame ... strengthening those who were weak ...

What word of healing and strengthening do you still need to hear from God? ... from others? ... Can you allow yourself to receive what the healing God would want to give your right now? ...

(ALLOW A LONG SILENCE.)

Gradually and gently draw yourself from this sacred space ... knowing that you may return whenever you need to ... Draw yourself from the meditation scene ... and gradually connect with this body-self that is you right now ... Make some gentle movements with your fingers and toes ... some movements with your neck ... Begin to notice your breath again ... this breath that has been breathing you all the time you have been meditating ... even if you have not paid attention to it ... As you are ready, open your eyes ...

Silence

Provide a time for journalling or drawing for those who find it helpful.

Ring the bell at the end of the silent time to call people into the group again.

Debriefing

Invite people to share their experience during the meditation and in particular to notice how God was with them in the meditation.

Closure

Name into the centre of the circle a word or phrase that describes how you experienced God being with you today.

MEDITATION

13

Philip and the Ethiopian Eunuch

A Meditation Inviting Us to Encounter Deeply Those Who Are Different from Us

Introduction

This meditation would be useful at a retreat or gathering where a congregation is working on inclusivity or welcoming strangers.

Preparation

- paper and pens for journalling
- CD player with appropriate background music
- bell to ring when shifting from writing to meditation
- worship space that evokes the desert
- bowl of water to evoke the baptism references in the scripture
- photos of people who are different from those who are normally in your congregation

Scripture

Acts 8:26–39

Reflection

This is a rather strange scripture as Philip seems to have magical powers that we read as quite bizarre. If you get beyond that, however, the real magic happens in the profound encounter Philip had with the man from Ethiopia.

In Acts, we meet Philip on the road leading from Jerusalem to Gaza (unfortunately a place we know of too well from current accounts of the Israeli-Palestinian conflict).

Scripture tells us that this was a wilderness road, which is significant because wilderness in scripture is where one time ends and another begins. Wilderness is where the Hebrews were formed into a people after they left Egypt during 40 years of their transforming journey ... getting lost ... getting found. Some people have called this "wilderness school." Wilderness is the place where individuals or a whole people experience being stripped of their masks and learned behaviours so that they become open to the God who transforms and calls. Wilderness is where Jesus went at the beginning of his ministry to discern his call.

When we hear the word "wilderness" in scripture, it often means a place where people will be open to a transforming experience with God. And this story is no exception. However, one wonders, Who was transformed most, Philip or the Eunuch from Ethiopia?

We are told that the Ethiopian eunuch had come to Jerusalem to worship. Now the interesting thing is that there was no way that this castrated man would have been allowed into the temple. There was a strict law forbidding it. So he had come all this way and been refused entry even though it does not say so in the text. Even so, this was a man of power serving a woman, Candace, Queen of the Ethiopians, and he was in charge of all of her wealth.

Philip has just come from Samaria, an area considered unclean by religious orthodoxy. It is the area that constitutes much of the West Bank today. There Philip has had great success proclaiming the kingdom of God. He seems to have had a few tricks up his sleeve, amazing them with magic, which perhaps helped to get their attention.

Philip has already crossed boundaries to go into Samaria and now he is led by the Spirit into the wilderness south of Jerusalem and told to approach a man who is a foreigner from Ethiopia, a man who is black, a man who is a eunuch. These were all qualities that would have rendered him "other," not one of ours, someone to avoid and be suspicious of.

This Ethiopian is a seeker, one who is already reading the scripture. As he sits in his chariot, he reads from the prophet Isaiah: "Like a sheep he was led to the slaughter, and like a lamb silent before his shearer, so he does not open his mouth. In his humiliation justice was denied him. Who can describe his generation? For his life was taken away from the earth." (Acts 8:32–33)

Now we are quick to read Jesus into this passage, but remember again who is reading this: a man whose fertility was taken from him, a man whose future generations were taken from the earth, a man who had just returned from Jerusalem where he had tried to worship and been turned away. He would certainly find himself in the words "in his humiliation justice was denied him."

Scripture comes alive for us when we recognize ourselves in it. We recognize our story in The Story. Surely this Ethiopian eunuch found himself in this scripture.

In the deep encounter, listening and sharing, Philip shares the story of Jesus. The Jesus story connected with the Ethiopian so much that when they found water in this desert (again a powerful metaphor), the Ethiopian, who had not been welcome at the temple, was welcomed into Christ's movement in baptism.

We have no idea what happened to him afterwards, but we do know that the Ethiopian church was one of the earliest and most powerful.

This is a profound story of a transforming love that called the early church to reach across boundaries of culture, race, sexuality, power. It is a profound story of what happens when we deeply encounter one another and share our stories of life and of God.

Gathering (Choose a, b, or c)

a) Share a time when you have felt not accepted by a group.

b) If you are part of a congregation or established group, ask the question: "Who would not be welcome in our congregation/group?" Since most groups perceive themselves to welcome "everyone," you might suggest some categories, such as recovering alcoholics or drug addicts, a gay or lesbian couple with or without children, a person suffering from mental illness, or someone who had been imprisoned for child abuse. Exploring–without being judgmental, but being honest–the limits of inclusivity is an important exercise for any group.

c) Share all or part of the Reflection as appropriate for your group.

Meditation

Close your eyes ... Become aware of this body-self that is you, as you come to meditation today ... Focus on your breath ... Notice the pattern of your breathing ... as it moves in ... as it moves out ... Notice how fast you are breathing ... Notice whether you are breathing deeply or with shallow breaths ... Notice where your body moves when you breathe ... Is the movement in your chest or in your belly? ...

Watch your breathing for a few minutes and notice any changes that occur ... You may find that just attending to your breath will allow you to relax ... As you focus and breathe let your breaths become slower and deeper ... Let your body relax and move to a sense of peace ...

Notice where your body is sore or tense ... Imagine the breath moving to that place ... and gently massaging the tightened knots of tension ... or fear ... or anger ... Simply allow the breath to open up your body ... so that your life energy can flow freely ... You are preparing yourself for prayer ...

As you focus on your breathing ... you may notice thoughts coming and going ... Just notice the thoughts, then let them go ... You may want to imagine them as clouds floating across the horizon ... or as leaves on a stream being carried away ... As thoughts arise, gently return your focus to your breath ... Notice the space that opens inside you as you relax ... as you gradually come into your sacred centre ...

As you come to that sacred centre ... the place where your core reality is connected with the Holy ... invite God's Spirit to lead you and guide you ... as you imagine yourself into the experience of the story ...

In the scripture ... the encounter between Philip and the Ethiopian man happened in the wilderness ... in a time of deep disappointment ... the Ethiopian eunuch had stopped his chariot ... perhaps to rest ... perhaps to nurse his wounds of rejection and disappointment ... perhaps just to reflect on how he could have been naive enough to believe that someone like him could be accepted by God ...

The eunuch from Ethiopia had heard that there was a sacred way to God in the far-off city of Jerusalem ... and had gone there to experience it ... and to worship ... He would not have been welcomed ... He was going away with a deep sense of loss ... and perhaps even humiliation ...

Let yourself be in touch with your own sense of wilderness ... Be in touch with your own experience of not being welcomed ... of having your hopes raised only to experience disappointment ... Be in touch with what it feels like to live outside the circle ... as one who is not seen ... as one who does not belong ... as one who is judged on the way you look ... on your sexual orientation ... on your history ... on whatever it is that makes you different ...

Now become the man from Ethiopia ... You had so hoped that this would be the place where you could find God ... You had heard such wonderful things about the God of Israel ... about the holy temple ... There may have been something there ... but it was not for you ... You thought you were coming to a God of justice and compassion ... but that had not been your experience when you were turned away by the priests at the temple ... "Our laws forbid it!" they had said ... "There is nothing we can do!" ... You are confused ...

But still you search ... Imagine yourself trying to read again the writings that are sacred to this faith ... not knowing if you are looking for something that will prove once and for all that it is a sham ... or if you are looking for truth ...

And then you see words that almost leap off the page ... words that name your condition as if someone had been inside your skin and written it ... Your experience of dejection ... your experience of your life being taken away from the earth when you were castrated ... This painful experience written in a holy book! ... These seem to be more than just words on a page ... They seem to be words that were meant just for you ... and you experience yourself as known by God ... seen by God ... exactly as you are ... known with compassion ... known with deep understanding ...

Then you notice a stranger ... someone you had not seen coming ... You expect the same kind of humiliation you have had in Jerusalem ... so you avert your eyes and stare off into the distance ...

But the stranger comes to you ... and asks if he can sit with you ... He asks what you are reading and if you understand it ... When you show him the words that have so spoken to your heart ... he listens ... and he understands ...

He shares with you the ancient stories of his faith ... stories of a God who sets free ... stories of a God who works through the lost ... the last ... the least ... He shares with you the stories of a man whose teaching has turned his world upside down ... This man touched lepers clean ... opened the eyes and hearts of those who tried to put a limit on God's love ... This man Jesus taught that God's love is for all ... especially those whom the religious authorities had judged as unclean and unworthy ...

He tells you that while this man was alive he did his best to transform his religion ... to reach out to those who had been excluded ... to let God go free from the prisons people had created for God ...

Now those who are left behind are called to do this ... to proclaim God's love ... and God's presence alive in all things ... alive in you ... God's love ... and God's presence alive in you ... right here in this wilderness ... You are known ... you are loved by the Sacred Source ... God's life is in you ... Your life is not limited by how others judge you ... You are loved by God ... and you are called to follow ... and share this love with all others ... You can hardly believe it ...

But as you journey along together ... deep in conversation and reflection ... you are given another sign ...

There is water ... healing water in the desert ... living water where you least expect it ... You allow this messenger of God to take you into the water ... where you feel the refreshing ... renewing ... coolness of the water pouring over you ... You allow yourself to be baptized into this new way of being in the world ... this new way of seeing yourself ... of seeing God ... this healing way ... this radical way of grace ...

Allow the waters of transformation and healing to pour over you again and again ... as you choose this new way of life in all its fullness ... Notice if there is anything the Spirit would like to say to you as you experience this ritual of transformation and healing ...

Gradually draw yourself away from this journey ... and connect with the body-self that is you today in this place ... Notice your breathing as you breathe in the goodness and grace of God ... Notice the feeling of your feet on the floor of your body in your chair ... Gradually make some gentle movement with your toes ... with your fingers ... with your shoulders ... as you allow yourself to reconnect with this place ... and open your eyes as you are ready ...

Silence

Provide a time for journalling or drawing for those who find it helpful.

Ring the bell at the end of the silent time to call people into the group again.

Debriefing

For Small Groups

Share wisdom gained from the experience of this meditation for your own life and the life of your community.

For Large Groups

a) Imagine what your congregation or group would be like if you were willing to go into the wilderness to meet those who had been turned away by traditional faith.

b) Who would you risk being with on your journey?

c) What good news of God's transforming love would you be able to share?

d) What would it mean to baptize these people into your community?

Closure

Share a word or phrase that describes how you have experienced God being with you today.

MEDITATION

14

Formed by God

Introduction

Preparation

- paper and pens for journalling
- pottery centre with potter's wheel and real clay, modelling clay, or Plasticine. You may invite a potter to come to the group to work on a wheel or by hand as you reflect on being formed by God
- worship centre with different clay objects, both practical and beautiful, and magazine photos of African or Latin American potters working their craft in the ancient way that would have been familiar to Jeremiah
- music for gathering or closure, such as "Abba Father,"[12] sung by the Reverend Carey Landry or "Earthen Vessels,"[13] sung by the St. Louis Jesuits that refers to a passage in Corinthians about treasure in earthen vessels. Available on cassette and CD
- CD player with appropriate background music
- bell to ring when shifting from writing to meditation

Scripture

Psalm 139, Jeremiah 18:1–11

Reflection

Both scriptures give us images of a God who takes a very intimate, hands-on approach to forming us and who knows us to the core. The psalmist says: "It was you who formed my inward parts; you knit me together in my mother's womb. I praise you, for I am fearfully and wonderfully made. Wondrous are your works that I know very well. My frame was not hidden from you, when I was being made in secret, intricately woven in the depths of the earth. Your eyes beheld my unformed substance ... How weighty to me are your thoughts, O God! How vast is the sum of them! I try to count them—they are more than the sand; I come to the end—I am still with you." (Psalm 139:13–18)

What would our lives be like if we could actually integrate and live out of this experience of a forming, shaping, intimately knowing, loving God? Not a God who is just an abstract concept, a God to fill up the empty spaces when we feel needy. But a vital, creating, life-making God, a connecting, creating energy that flows through all of life. A God who knew us before our days on earth and who is with us long after our death. A God who is spoken of in The United Church of Canada's "A New Creed," particularly in the line "In life, in death, in life beyond death, God is with us. We are not alone. Thanks be to God."[14]

In the passage from Jeremiah, this creating God is met by Jeremiah while he is watching a potter at work, hands on the clay, bending carefully over the pot being created. Jeremiah recognizes God as the potter and the people as the clay.

I was a potter for nine years before becoming a minister. There is profound spiritual wisdom in the process of creating from clay.

Clay comes from the earth. Though these days most potters buy clay already prepared, in biblical times, and still in many places, potters dig and prepare their own clay. Before a potter can work the clay, there is a lengthy preparation phase. The clay must be cleansed of all twigs and rocks, then soaked to create an even consistency, then allowed to mellow.

Following this it is wedged, which is a process of working the clay by throwing and kneading it until all of the particles come together into a whole and all of the air bubbles are removed. There are parts of the clay that have different consistencies. Wedging the clay integrates all of these parts into a whole that can be worked.

Even before there can be any moulding of the clay, there has been a lot of work done by the potter, lots of loving attention given to preparing and getting ready to create.

At this point, the clay is ready to be formed into something of worth. The potter needs to know the clay so that he or she can choose the right clay for the particular process of creation. Some clay is better for working with by hand. Other clay is better for throwing on a wheel. The potter chooses the clay that is ripe, ready, and well-prepared for the particular task the potter is planning.

For a thrown pot, the potter puts the clay on the wheel and begins the process of centring. Unless the clay is centred precisely, the pot created will be lopsided or may even come apart on the wheel. It requires gentle but firm pressure, sensitive concentration, and intuitive knowing by the potter in order to centre the clay. Coming to centre is the first part of the process of working with clay on a wheel.

Only at this point can the clay be opened and gradually lifted up to form the pot. The potter needs to put exactly the right amount of water on the clay during this process, so that the hands move easily and freely on the clay, but not so much that it takes away the strength of the clay. The pressure and support come from the inside and the outside. With too much pressure in either direction, the pot is thrown off centre and the potter must begin again.

Once the walls of the pot are shaped and lifted up, the pot is cut off the wheel and placed to dry. It must do so in just the right conditions, carefully tended. If it dries too quickly or unevenly, cracks may appear.

At any point up to this next stage, the clay can be soaked and wedged again, then reworked. It is very fragile and can hold no liquid without simply melting back to its original clay.

It is in the firing that the pot is formed permanently. Fire strengthens the clay, so that all the particles come together into a whole. It tests the integrity of the creation and if there are hidden air bubbles, it will crack. It is in the fire that the pot becomes what it is meant to be. For most pots, this is done in stages: first comes a forming fire, called bisque firing. Then comes a glazing fire, heated to a much higher temperature, where the coating that gives the pot the colour and beautiful surface is formed.

The pot is now ready for use: to contain, to pour out, to hold, to empty, to store good things, to be an object of beauty and worth.

It was in watching the potter lovingly at work over the creation that Jeremiah understood the creating, recreating God.

Gathering

a) Read or refer to the scripture (one or both).

b) Share the Reflection with the group or give a brief resume in your own words so that others understand the process of creating with clay. Ask members of the group to notice if any part of the metaphor connects with them at this time in their life.

c) Even if you are unable to have a potter present, you may be able to obtain some clay that people could handle as they gather and reflect.

d) Where do you have a sense of God forming you at this time in your life?

Meditation

Have journals and writing tools ready for use at the end of the meditation.

Close your eyes ... Become aware of this body-self that is you, as you come to meditation today ... Focus on your breath ... Notice the pattern of your breathing ...as it moves in ... as it moves out ... Follow your breath in ... Follow your breath out ... Notice how fast you are breathing ... Notice whether you are breathing deeply or with shallow breaths ... Notice where your body moves when you breathe ... Is the movement in your chest ...or in your belly? ...

Watch your breathing for a few minutes ...notice any changes that occur ... You may find that just attending to your breath will allow you to relax ... As you focus and breathe, let your breaths become slower and deeper ... Let your body relax and move to a place of peace ...

Notice where your body is sore or tense ... Imagine the breath moving to that place ...and gently massaging the tightened knots of tension ... or fear ...or anger ... or stress ... Simply allow the breath to open up your body ... so that your life energy can flow freely ... You are preparing yourself for prayer.

As you focus on your breathing ... you may notice thoughts coming and going ... Just notice the thoughts ... then let them go ... You may want to imagine them as clouds floating across the horizon ...or as leaves on a stream being carried away ... As thoughts arise ...gently return your focus to your breath ... Notice the space that opens inside you as you relax ... as you gradually come into your sacred centre ...

Ask God to bless this meditation journey and to use it for your highest good of mind ... body ... and spirit ...

In your sacred centre, I invite you to imagine yourself as clay ... on a bank beside a river ... You are simply part of the earth ... Notice the kind of clay you are ... Are you a delicate, fine clay ... suitable for creating elegant china ... or are you a more earth-toned clay? ... Are you smooth ... or do you have a more gritty texture? ... Notice the colour of the clay you are ... Notice what it feels like to lie dormant as the clay that you are ... full of potential ... yet unused ...

Be in touch with the experience of being chosen by the potter ... the one who has seen the potential in you ... and has seen the possibility of what you could become ...

Imagine the potter going through the process of preparing the clay ... digging ... sifting ... soaking ... wedging ... removing what gets in the way ...

If you reflect on your own life as clay ... notice how the potter God has lovingly prepared you ... worked in your life to this point ... so that you are ready for being formed ...

Remember sifting, cleansing times ... when you have let go of parts of yourself that were no longer useful ...

Remember dormant, waiting times ...when the work was going on internally ...without much outward sign ...

In your imagination ... get a sense of where God is trying to form you now ... Are you in the stage of being centred ... of being lovingly ... but firmly ... challenged to find your centre so that you can grow into what you are meant to be? ...

Are you being opened ... gradually lifted up as you are supported? ... Notice the gentle pressure and support ... both from the inside and the outside ... pressure and support to grow ... to change ... to become what God would have you be ... what you were always intended to be.... Where are the pressures in your life from within and from without? ... Are they balanced or unequal?

Are you in a time of passing through the fire ... in a testing time ... a time of strengthening your integrity? ... The potter knows when the clay is ready to enter the fire of transformation ... Where are you experiencing this kind of transformation in your life? ... This kind of strengthening? ...

Do you have a sense of what God is creating you to be ... what God's intention for you might be? ...

Sit in silence for a while as you reflect on this process ... Be in touch with the God who creates ... the God who forms ... the God who transforms ... and notice where you are being formed by God at this time in your life ...

When you are ready ... gradually draw yourself back to this space ... staying in sacred space ... as you write or draw your response to this meditation in your journal.

Silence

Provide a time for journalling or drawing for those who find it helpful.

Ring the bell at the end of the silent time to call people into the group again.

Debriefing

a) Invite people to share, as they are able, what happened for them in this time of meditative prayer.

b) If you have clay, you may wish to have people work with it now. If they worked on it at the beginning of the session in reflection and gathering time, they may have some insights about what they have created and may wish to share with the group.

Closure

Close with a brief prayer of thanksgiving.

MEDITATION

15

The Breath of Life

A Meditation for Those in Exile

Introduction

This meditation can be used for worship or individual use. It is also useful for a congregation in the process of discerning its spiritual health or facing changing times.

Preparation

- paper and pens for journalling
- worship centre with candle, images of desert and exile, bones (if possible)
- CD player and appropriate background music
- bell to ring when shifting from writing to meditation
- Read carefully the scripture and Reflection below. You will need to share the material in the Reflection by reading or paraphrasing it in your own words.

Scripture

Ezekiel 37:1–14

Reflection[15]

Many in the church identify with Walter Brueggemann's prophetic analysis that we are a people in exile. (See Bibliography, page 179, for books written by Brueggemann.) He has done brilliant theological reflection on our times using the biblical metaphor of exile:

- Exile is when one time is over and another has not yet begun.

- Exile is when the familiar place, where you belonged and knew the rules, is no longer possible, but you have not yet found a new way to make home.
- Exile is a place where you are forced to learn to live in a brand new reality that you did not necessarily choose, but to which you have to adjust.
- Exile is a place where how we identified ourselves and understood ourselves no longer works. We are forced to reinvent ourselves and figure out who we are in this new world.
- Exile is also where we recognize that our own resources, our own abilities to control our situation, have reached their limits, and where we are forced to rely on the radical freedom of God's Spirit.
- Exile is where the people of God were reformed, recreated, and where faith and theology took new directions.

I have to agree with Walter Brueggemann in that we have much to learn from the biblical metaphor and experience of exile.

Exile is not something you fix, using problem-solving tools, which we are so good at doing in the church. It is a whole new ball game, where we have to learn new things, new ways to live, and to be open to the Spirit's leading. This is the only way we are going to pass through it.

Ezekiel 37:1–14 is a powerful story of the Spirit moving through the life of a courageous leader, in a community in one of the worst times in Jewish history. The scene is Babylon, six centuries before Christ.

In those days, there were kingdoms rising and falling; there always are. There were nations that abused power; there always are. And the skinny little strip of land that was Israel always seemed to be directly in the path of these strong, expanding nations that surrounded it.

First the Assyrians gobbled up the northern kingdom of Israel in one voracious bite, spewing out refugees across the then known world. One hundred years later, Nebuchadnezzar, King of Babylon, did a power dance on the border of the southern kingdom, creating terror and extorting heavy reparation payments in return for security. But he invaded anyway.

He and his army forces marched the leaders—religious, political, and cultural—across the barren wastes into Babylon (modern-day Iraq). Many died of exhaustion and hardship on the way to Babylon.

Ezekiel was a young priest who was carried off in the first wave of captives in 587 BCE. It was while he was in exile that he received his call to be a prophet.

Biblical prophecy is not so much about foretelling the future, but more about reading the signs of the times and speaking God's truth into the situation.

A year later, Ezekiel heard that Jerusalem had been captured and the temple, where he had served as priest, was in ashes. More exiles from Jerusalem were herded up and taken to Babylon. This news plunged the exiles into deep despair and hopelessness. Already they were uprooted, strangers in a strange land. Their political, economic, cultural, and religious life was over. Now their beloved Jerusalem was in ruin, the temple destroyed. It felt like a reverse exodus from freedom to slavery.

It is impossible to overstate the deep trauma that the events of 587 produced in Jerusalem. It was a public, political, and military event, but it was also a profound theological crisis.

Questions haunted the exiles: Is God powerful any longer? Is God no longer faithful? Is there any future for this community?

Destabilization and displacement produced deep grief.

And so the story begins in spiritual death. Grief is acknowledged. There is no denial, no masks. The despair is named and honoured. It is summed up in the exiles' cry "Our bones are dry, our thread of life is snapped, our web is severed from the loom."[16]

Beneath it lurks the existential groan: "Is there any hope?" "Can these bones live?" This is a hard place to be; an end-of-the rope place to be.

Just when it seems that all is beyond hope, God gives Ezekiel a vision. This vision helps Ezekiel capture the essence of the condition of the people; to see them as a valley of dried out, disconnected bones, dislocated, lifeless, with no energy, no power, no capacity to relate or connect. In the vision, Ezekiel sees God bringing new life to the people; life beyond how things are now.

It is the Word of God that Ezekiel speaks into the deadness of the people that will renew them. God will repeat the moment of creation when human beings received God's breath of life, the breath of God's Spirit. The word *ruah*, same as at creation, appears 14 times in this passage.

But this re-creation doesn't happen right away. The bones have to come together, to rattle and struggle up against each other. They make a terrific racket while they are doing this in this story. And the bones themselves are not enough.

There needs to be sinew to bind them together, and muscles. There needs to be some hard, painful work before the breath of life (which is called from the four directions: the east, the south, the west, the north) can come upon them that they may live.

But the promise is clear that God's life-making Spirit will take their deadness, their dryness, their brittleness, and bring new life.

This is not just an individual resurrection from personal despair. It is about community. The separated bones will come together as a people. What seemed like death and the end of their relationship with God was instead a time of reorientation, of dying to an old way and rising to a new.

Little did the exiles know at the time that this 50-year period, which seemed like ending times, this time without a temple structure, would later be described as the most formative of their history after the Exodus. When the people, with the help of the prophets, integrated the exile into their collective psyche, they saw it as a time for repentance (turning around), a time of reflection and of reorientation. Instead of just being an ending, it became the beginning of a new era, a time when they learned to grow beyond the image of a national protector God. They came to experience a God who was present wherever they were, a God beyond strict religious systems, a God of presence and consolation.

During this time, much of the Hebrew scripture's oral tradition was written down and gathered together. By remembering the stories of their experience of God in the past, the people reconnected with hope. Exile was a time when the synagogue, small communities of followers not tied to a central temple, was established. All of this has been foundational for modern Judaism.

It is a good reminder for us in our times of dislocation, when systems and structures are crumbling that, wherever we are at any particular point in the process, this is not the end of the journey, but merely one vantage point along the way. God may be doing some brand new thing that we have not even begun to catch sight of or to imagine.

Gathering

For Small Groups

a) Share whatever part of the Reflection you feel is useful.

b) Read the story from *The New English Bible*, entering the feeling of the passage. This meditation assumes a familiarity with the movements of the story, so it is important that the group be in touch with the dynamics of the biblical story.

c) Invite the group to take a moment to let the story find its home in them.

Where do you find yourself in this story today? Where do you find your congregation in this story today?

For Community Discernment

If you are using this meditation for community discernment, read the Reflection or share it in your own words. Invite the group to form small groups and read the scripture from the *The New English* version of the Bible. Invite them to notice where they find themselves in the story.

a) Where do you have to acknowledge that the way things were is no longer possible?

b) Where are you living the uncertainty and chaos of the transition time when one way is over and another has not yet begun?

c) Where are you experiencing a new breath coming into your community life, perhaps from outside, as does the breath in the Ezekiel passage?

d) What new breath is God trying to breathe into your life as a community?

e) Where is the new breath causing struggle?

After this discussion, lead the meditation, which will take the same questions to a deeper level of listening to the Spirit. Ask the members of the group to listen for what the Spirit wants to say to their community through this meditation.

If used for discernment of the spiritual life of a community, I have placed in parentheses the optional references to community life.

Meditation

Close your eyes ... Notice what it feels like to be in this body-self that is you right now ... Most of us go through our whole days, sometimes whole lives ... without paying attention to this body-self ... In Hebrew (the language system Jesus knew) ... there was no such thing as disembodied spirit ... They spoke of the *nephesh* ... the body soul ... the spirit body ... Jesus talked about our bodies as temples of the Spirit ... What is it like for you to think of yourself in that way? ...

As you begin to pay attention to your body, do you notice places where tension is stored up ... places where your muscles are in tight knots? ... As you scan your body ... from the top of your head to the bottom of your feet ... notice if there are tender places ... and send compassion to these places in your body ... thanking them for the hard work they are doing ... You might offer to pay more attention to what they are telling you in the future ...

Become aware of your breathing ... this life-giving process that goes on all of the time ... even when we are not conscious of it ... Notice if you are breathing with only a small part of your lungs ... or whether you are taking the breath deeply into your whole being ... down to the bottom of your lungs ... up to the tops of your shoulders ... Notice if your tummy moves in and out as you inhale and as you exhale ... This is how a baby breathes when it is breathing naturally ... before its body has become tensed and locked up with the stress of living ...

Let your body relax ... opening to the breath of life ... Let the tension flow out of your body through your feet ... Begin to allow your breath to move deeper into your being ...

Take the breath deep down into your belly ... Breathe in deeply the healing presence of God ... the goodness and grace of God ... Take it right into the core of your being ... As you breathe out ... let the breath carry with it the poisons ... physical ... emotional ... spiritual ... that have built up in your system ... Breathe in the newness of possibility ... Breathe in the hope that God gives ... Let go of the stress and tensions that are stored in your body-self ... in your emotional self ... in your spiritual self ... Breathe in life energy ... the creating breath of God that was there from the beginning ... Breathe out whatever would block you from being fully present to this time ...

Again, notice your body ... If there are still tense places, imagine this healing breath moving directly to those spots ... loosening the tension ... letting go ... letting be ... letting open ... letting unlock ... Know that you are in a safe place ...

Notice the inner space that is being prepared and opened up inside you ... space for the sacred presence to find room ... space for the Holy One to be with you ... your own sacred space ... your own holy ground ...

Ask God to bless this meditation journey ... and to use it for your highest good of mind ... body ... and spirit ...

I invite you to imagine your life through the metaphor of the valley of dry bones ... God needed Ezekiel to look honestly at the situation in which his people found themselves ... He had to be "real" about the world in which he found himself ... There was no denial ... He was led by the Spirit to go to and fro, to and fro, through the valley of bones ...

As you look honestly at your own life (or the life or your community) ... are you at a "dried bones time" in your life? ... Are there places of deep loss? ... Are there places where everything feels dislocated ... dry ... lifeless? ... Are there places where you need to break through a wall of denial about how things really are? ... Simply be with that place in your life, asking the Spirit to offer you wisdom.

(LONG SILENCE)

Or maybe you are at a different place in your life? ... Are you just beginning to hear the Word of God evoking new life in you? ... How is that happening? ... What does that new life need in order to grow? ... Are you being invited into a new phase of your life? ... Is there anything you can do to allow it to come to fullness?

(LONG SILENCE)

Or is your life at a place where the Spirit is beginning to rattle up the bones against each other ... but you are still not in touch with the life breath? ...

Is your life feeling disconnected ... disjointed ... not yet integrated? ... Is there conflict? ... Can you trust that the Spirit is working in you and that this is part of the process?

(LONG SILENCE)

Or are you feeling the coming together of the parts ... the knitting together of the separate pieces ... the putting of flesh ... of muscle ... of strength on the hard, dried bones?

(LONG SILENCE)

Where are you feeling the life-giving breath of the Spirit in your life right now (in the life of your community)? ... Where are you experiencing your hope being renewed? ... Where are you feeling restored to aliveness ... to vitality ... to wholeness?

(LONG SILENCE)

Ask God to offer you what you need in your life right now (or in the life of your community).

When you feel ready ... gradually draw yourself back to this place ... Notice your breath ... Notice your body-self as it is sitting in the chair ... Feel the bottom of your feet as they connect you with the earth ... Gradually make some gentle movements with your toes and fingers ... some circles with your shoulders and head ... When you are ready ... open your eyes.

Silence

Take as much time as people need to write in their journals or to integrate the meditation quietly.

Ring the bell at the end of the silent time to call people into the group again.

Debriefing

For Community Discernment

If you are using this meditation for community discernment, invite each person in the circle to name what she or he believes the Spirit wants to say to the community through this meditation. Where did you hear, feel, or intuit some insight from the Spirit for the community?

You might want to facilitate this by passing a stone or other item around the circle. Each person would share in turn or pass prayerfully if he or she has nothing to say.

For the Group

If you are using the meditation for individual spiritual growth, invite members of the group to share, as they feel called, the insights they had during the meditation.

Closure

Share the following prayer.

> Spirit of God, breathe us with your breath of life.
>
> Breathe new life into our sagging souls.
>
> Breathe hope into our despair.
>
> Breathe order into our chaos.

Breathe compassion into our impatience.

Breathe surprise into our complacency.

Breathe joy into our heaviness.

Breathe life into our dried out places

that we might live.

Amen.

Part V

Meditations for Spiritual and Personal Growth

MEDITATION

16

Moving Beyond the Blame Game

Introduction

Meditation 16, either alone or in conjunction with Meditation 17, could form the basis of a retreat on personal spiritual growth.

Preparation

- paper and pens for journalling
- CD player with appropriate background music
- bell to ring when shifting from writing to meditation
- worship centre with pictures or articles of people in disagreement and people reconciling

Read the Reflection carefully and all of the scriptures referred to. Then immerse yourself in the dynamic of the meditation. Particularly note the caveat about those who are at the beginning of a healing journey from abuse.

Scripture

Luke 6:37–42

Reflection

Scripture is full of examples of Jesus teaching his disciples to move beyond the blame game, for example, in Luke 11:33–36, Luke 9:1–56, Luke 7:36–50, and quintessentially in Luke 6:37–42, the Sermon on the Mount, where Jesus asks:

"Can a blind person guide a blind person?" He seems to suggest that for us to be "fully qualified" as his followers, as spiritual teachers like him, we have to learn not only to focus on the speck in our neighbour's eye, but also to notice the log in our own eye. We have to see clearly with eyes that are unobstructed by our own blind spots.

As I write this, I am aware of a broad continuum in the movement towards forgiveness. I have worked closely with those who have experienced abuse. For those at a very beginning stage of this journey there is much self-blame and feelings that "Everything is my fault." At this stage, spiritual growth and healing mean being able to name the wrongdoing of others, recognizing that you are not to blame for what has happened to you while you were vulnerable. It is important to be able to recognize that you were unable to make a free choice. The healing path at that stage of the journey is growing into a clear self, separate and apart from the abused self. It is important to see yourself as so much more than what has happened to you.

This meditation is not meant for people at this early stage of their spiritual journey. It would be more appropriate, using the imagery of the scripture, to do a meditation that removes the log of blame that has been placed onto the self. For there is still blindness that blocks clear, whole seeing.

But there are far more of us who cling to the blaming of others and hang on to victimization in a way that keeps us blind to our own personal shadow. It is impossible for us to gain wholeness and wisdom if we do not know ourselves deeply, including our shadow selves. Carl Jung's psychology reminds us that wholeness comes from integration, and that owning the energy in the shadow is an essential part of that growth towards wholeness.

The shadow is the unlived, unacknowledged part of our lives. When we deeply admire another person or when we are triggered into deep dislike, Jung would invite us to pay careful attention.

We need to notice what we are drawn to in admiration (the positive unlived shadow) and what we hate in the other (the negative unlived shadow). As we do this, we will often discover a part of ourselves of which we have been unconscious. The challenge then is to befriend this part of ourselves, to bring it to consciousness, to integrate it in a healthy way. This frees the energy that it holds for the fullness of our living. Along our path, ending the blame game is one of the movements of the Spirit.

Blame is one way of keeping ourselves in the prison of unconscious living and, when we live that way, we create havoc in our personal relationships and in our working lives without knowing what we are doing. I have met people who have a sense that the whole world is against them because the same negative experiences keep happening to them. All the while, they are completely blind to how their own actions, approaches, or choices are in fact creating the very situations in which they are blaming others.

There are payoffs to the blame game. You get to feel superior. You get to direct the focus of attention away from yourself and your own insecurities and failings. You get to feel righteous. Perhaps if you point the finger, justice will be done. If justice is not done, you can assume the role of the unjustly aggrieved person.

Blaming has a valid place in the legal system. When people break the law, they should be identified and take responsibility for their actions. However, even then, many recognize that often there is a better way in a restorative justice approach that looks to restoring relationships as well as taking responsibility.

For a lot of us, blaming is an overused tool in our emotional repertoire. Normally, we learn to blame early in life. As we develop our sense of right and wrong, we identify wrongdoers around us. As a mother of two sons, I can remember the days when one brother would come to tell me what the other had done in the hopes that I, the source of all power, would be the judge to restore justice and soothe a tiny, affronted ego.

As we grow up, we continue to use blame to clarify the good from the bad in our world. We may come to believe that when we blame people we are providing a service. We feel we are making the world safer by shining the light of justice on transgressors. (Some people even make it a national policy.) At the same time, we may be meeting our own neurotic agenda of transferring awareness of the source of our bad feelings to an external cause: if I feel bad and I can blame you, I don't need to take responsibility for my bad feelings.

But there are serious problems attached to blaming. It creates an either/or dynamic in relationships. Either you are with me or against me. It locks us and others in a power struggle to protect our self-esteem. It prevents us from really knowing the other, since we assume guilt and negative motivation in the other and relate to them through that projected image. It keeps us blind to our own faults and our own role in the conflict, whether intentional or unintentional. It keeps us from knowing the fullness of our own humanity, and from growing into a responsible, mature, integrated person who is comfortable acknowledging that we sometimes make mistakes.

We all have faults and failings. We all have a shadow side that contains parts of our self-image that we can't bear to look at. Looking deeply into that shadow makes us less likely to blame others. Knowing our own weaknesses gives us more tolerance for the weaknesses of others.

As we own and acknowledge and become compassionate with all parts of our selves, we allow God to create and heal in the wholeness of who we are, not just in the "shiny" parts that we proudly show to the world. It is the path to freedom and responsible, mature spiritual living.

Gathering

Option 1

Read Luke 6:37-42 as a *lectio divina*. This particular form of *lectio divina* has been called the African Bible Study since Western theologians discovered it being used in a missiological institute in South Africa. However, it is used in Christian base communities in Latin America and has long been used by Jesuits and other contemplatives as a form of prayer.

Explain the whole process (see below) that includes three readings with different questions. Remind people that *lectio divina* is about listening with the whole being for the way God would speak to us today through the scripture. It is a form of prayer. It is not analytical discussion or Bible study.

After each reading, there is silence, then people are invited to offer into the centre any insight they have heard with no discussion. Then proceed to the next reading.

1) Invite people to note a word, phrase, or image that stays with them while reading the passage.

   Read the passage through once slowly.

   Allow a time of silence.

   Invite sharing.

2) Invite people to reflect on how this passage connects with something in their own life experience.

   Read the passage again (perhaps by someone of a different gender).

Allow a time of silence.

Invite sharing.

3) Invite people to listen for where God might be challenging them or our world with a word of life or growth through the passage.

Read the passage again (perhaps by a third voice).

Allow a time of silence.

Invite sharing.

You may choose to close with the Lord's Prayer.

Option 2

Share what feels useful from the Reflection with the group and discuss one of the following questions.

a) Have you ever had the experience of recognizing that the quality you most disliked in another was, in fact, a part of yourself that you did not want to acknowledge?
b) Have you ever been the subject of projection, i.e. of being seen by another person in ways that have nothing to do with who you are?
c) Can you share an experience of being caught in the blame game (on either side)? What did you learn from that experience that can help us grow?

Meditation

This is a meditation that involves writing at various points, so participants should have a pen and paper ready as they go through the meditation.

Close your eyes ... Become aware of this body-self that is you, as you come to meditation today ... Focus on your breath ... Notice the pattern of your breathing ... as it moves in ... as it moves out ... Follow your breath in ... Follow your breath out ... Notice how fast you are breathing ... Notice whether you are breathing deeply or with shallow breaths ... Notice where your body moves when you breathe ... Is the movement in your chest ... or in your belly? ...

Watch your breathing for a few minutes ... Notice any changes that occur ... You may find that just attending to your breath will allow you to relax ... As you focus and breathe, let your breaths become slower and deeper ... Let your body relax and move to a place of peace ...

Notice where your body is sore or tense ... Imagine the breath moving to that place ... and gently massaging the tightened knots of tension ... or fear ... or anger ... or stress ... Simply allow the breath to open up your body ... so that your life energy can flow freely ... You are preparing yourself for prayer.

As you focus on your breathing ... you may notice thoughts coming and going ... Just notice the thoughts ... then let them go ... You may want to imagine them as clouds floating across the horizon ... or as leaves on a stream being carried away ... As thoughts arise ... gently return your focus to your breath ... Notice the space that opens inside you as you relax ... as you gradually come into your sacred centre ... space for the Holy One to be with you ... your own sacred space ... your own holy ground ... In this sacred centre ... invite God's Spirit to accompany you in this time of prayer ...

Imagine that you are in a sacred place that is safe and very special to you ... a place where you know yourself to be known and unconditionally loved by God ... As you are in this place ... call to mind a person who has qualities with whom you have great difficulty ... It does not need to be the most difficult person in your life ... In your imagination, you may choose to have the person kept very far away from you ... and you may choose to create whatever protection you need in order to feel safe ...

Allow the Spirit to offer you the insight into which person you should choose at this time ... Notice all of the things about this person that you detest ... Take some time to really notice all the qualities and behaviours that make up this dislike of the person you have chosen ...

When you are in touch with these behaviours, still staying in sacred space, write them down on your sheets of paper ...

(WRITING TIME; RING BELL TO SIGNAL THE END OF WRITING TIME)

Once you have written down all that you can think of at this time ... look over your notes as lovingly as you possibly can ... Invite God's Spirit to help you take a long, loving look ... noticing whether any of these qualities are part of your own make-up ...

It may be that they are qualities that you feel a tendency towards, but fight hard to keep under control ... It may be that there are sides of yourself that you do not know at all ... Don't force yourself to apply every aspect of the other person to yourself ... but listen for and notice those qualities that invite you to acknowledge and recognize in yourself ... Try not to move into self-blame as you do this ... Allow God's compassion to call out your own ... for loving acknowledgement and acceptance is where growth can begin ...

Pray with this as you listen to where God would nudge you ... Still staying in sacred space ... write down any wisdom you receive ...

(WRITING TIME; RING BELL TO SIGNAL THE END OF WRITING TIME)

When you have finished writing ... close your eyes again and as you are able ... surround this journey and your insights with healing light ... bathing yourself in compassion ... If you are able, let that light of compassion move from your centre to surround the other person who has unknowingly been your teacher today ... Notice if you see the other person differently because of the work you have done today ...

When you feel ready ... gradually draw yourself back to this place ... Notice your breath ... Notice your body-self as it is sitting in the chair ... Feel the bottom of your feet as they connect you with the earth ... Gradually make some gentle movements with your toes and fingers ... some circles with your shoulders and head ... When you are ready open your eyes ...

Silence

Debriefing

If your group is large, you may wish to invite sharing in pairs, since there may be sensitive material.

Closure

Invite the whole group to name how the Spirit was working with them today and to call out the word or phrase into the centre as a form of gathering prayer. End this prayer by thanking the Spirit in whatever way is comfortable for you and your group.

MEDITATION

17

Owning the Positive Shadow

A Companion Meditation

Introduction

Preparation

- paper and pens for journalling
- CD player with appropriate background music
- bell to ring when shifting from writing to meditation
- worship centre with pictures of people feeling good about themselves

Read the whole meditation and note the option of using a paper sheet attached to the back of each participant in the debriefing section. If this feels like a good idea for your group, provide paper, markers, and tape. The debriefing and closing rituals of this session are particularly important, so make sure you leave lots of time for this part of the session.

Read the Reflection and all of the scriptures carefully so that you immerse yourself in understanding the dynamic of the meditation.

Scripture

Isaiah 43:19, Isaiah 45:3

Reflection

Much has been written about coming to terms with the negative shadow and recognizing how we project it onto others if we are not conscious of it. Not as much emphasis has been placed on owning and integrating the positive shadow. Both are necessary parts of the journey to spiritual wholeness. According to Jung, the shadow is ALL the unlived, unacknowledged part of ourselves, which includes the negative as well as the positive.

There is unlived potential in all our lives. Many of us are unconscious of that unlived potential. When we are not owning the fullness of who we are, that energy can also create problems for us. We can become jealous and judgmental of others who have developed the very qualities we have left fallow. We begin to idolize those who have lived fully the qualities we have ignored. It can leave us as bitter people living much smaller lives than God intends for us.

Those who do not own their positive shadow can be vulnerable to strong charismatic leaders. They can project onto a religious leader, Jesus included, the spirituality, holiness, and justice-making that they are not developing in their own lives.

In reading scripture, I have been so impressed with how Jesus seems to turn people away from worshipping or adulating him, always turning them towards God and their own relationship with God. He seems to keep calling people to follow, but he calls them to live their own lives in faithfulness as he lived his life, rather than attach themselves to him in hero-worship. For me, this is a call to acknowledge our own unlived sacred shadow, to claim and live the Christ in us.

I have noticed that when people fall into romantic attraction, sometimes what is happening is the projection of the positive shadow onto another person. One recognizes parts of the self that are undeveloped and one is drawn irresistibly to those qualities in another. When we find ourselves drawn in admiration to another person, we should ask whether we are drawn to this person for the person, or for qualities that we are being invited to develop in our own lives. It can save some unhealthy romantic entanglements, as well as enable us to listen for the call to develop the fullness of life that God intends for us.

God truly is the genius of the indirect and uses all kinds of experiences to nudge us into wholeness (in biblical language, salvation).

Gathering

Option 1

Read the scripture as a *lectio divina.* (For an explanation of *lectio divina* see page 90 or 134.)

Option 2

Share and discuss the Reflection or one of the following questions:

a) Have you ever had the experience of recognizing that the quality you most admired in another was, in fact, a part of yourself that you did not want to acknowledge?

b) Have you ever been the subject of "projection," that is, of being seen by another person in ways that have nothing to do with who you are?

c) Write down the qualities you most admire in others. Now look at each of these qualities and notice if they are an unacknowledged part of you.

Meditation

This meditation involves some writing. Have pens and paper available.

Close your eyes ... Become aware of this body-self that is you, as you come to meditation today ... Focus on your breath ... Notice the pattern of your breathing ... as it moves in ... as it moves out ... Follow your breath in ... Follow your breath out ... Notice how fast you are breathing ... Notice whether you are breathing deeply or with shallow breaths ... Notice where your body moves when you breathe ... Is the movement in your chest ... or in your belly? ...

Watch your breathing for a few minutes ... Notice any changes that occur ... You may find that just attending to your breath will allow you to relax ... As you focus and breathe, let your breaths become slower and deeper ... Let your body relax and move to a place of peace ...

Notice where your body is sore or tense ... Imagine the breath moving to that place ... and gently massaging the tightened knots of tension ... or fear ... or anger ... or stress ... Simply allow the breath to open up your body ... so that your life energy can flow freely ... You are preparing yourself for prayer.

As you focus on your breathing ... you may notice thoughts coming and going ... Just notice the thoughts ... then let them go ... You may want to imagine them as clouds floating across the horizon ... or as leaves on a stream being carried away ... As thoughts arise ... gently return your focus to your breath ...

Notice the inner space that is being prepared and opened up inside you ... space for the sacred presence to find room ... space for the Holy One to be with you ... your own sacred space ...your own holy ground ...

Imagine that you are in a sacred place that is safe and very special to you ... a place where you know yourself to be known ... and unconditionally loved by God ... As you are in this place ... call to mind a person or persons with qualities that you really admire ...

Allow the Spirit to offer you the insight into the person you should choose at this time ... Notice all of the things about this person that you admire ... Take some time to notice all the qualities and behaviours that make up that admiration ... When you are in touch with these behaviours, still staying in sacred space, write them down on your sheets of paper ...

(WRITING TIME; RING BELL TO SIGNAL THE END OF WRITING TIME)

Once you have written down all that you can think of at this time, look over your notes as lovingly as you possibly can ... Invite God's Spirit to help you take a long, loving look at whether any of these qualities are part of your own make-up ... You may feel a tendency towards these qualities, but are afraid to acknowledge them ... There may be sides of yourself that you do not know at all ... Don't force yourself to apply every aspect of the other person to yourself ... but listen for and notice those qualities that you are being invited to acknowledge and recognize in yourself ... Try not to move into a judgment of yourself as you do this ... Allow God's compassion to call out your own ... for loving acknowledgement and acceptance is where growth can begin ... Pray with this as you listen to where God would nudge you ... Still staying in sacred space, write down any wisdom you receive ...

(WRITING TIME; RING BELL TO SIGNAL THE END OF WRITING TIME)

When you have finished writing ... close your eyes again and as you are able ... surround this journey and your insights with healing light ... bathing yourself in compassion ... If you are able ... let that light of compassion move from your centre to surround the other person who has unknowingly been your teacher today ... Notice if you see the other person any differently because of the work you have done today ...

When you feel ready ... gradually draw yourself back to this place ... Notice your breath ... Notice your body-self as it is sitting in the chair ... Feel the bottom of your feet as they connect you with the earth ... Gradually make some gentle movements with your toes and fingers ... some circles with your shoulders and head ... When you are ready, open your eyes ...

Debriefing

a) You may share in pairs if your group is large. However, if you have a trusting group, it would be wonderful for everyone to be heard as they share positive parts of themselves that they have just begun to recognize. You may help them by asking them to list the qualities on paper so that they can read these positive qualities aloud and have those characteristics witnessed by others.

This is one of the rare occasions after meditation when positive feedback is especially helpful. While listening to a person sharing, people can point out positive qualities in that person.

Positive mirroring, showing the beauty, truth, and goodness that is in us, is a rare experience. It is particularly rare for people to share this in a public setting. How sad that it is often only after people are dead that there is public thanksgiving for their lives. Only then will they be eulogized and praised for who they were. To have this happen while we are still alive is a powerful, moving experience of healing. Make sure you make space for this important part of the process.

b) Make sure that the person leaves with a concrete list of all the positive qualities. When we are receiving positive feedback and are not used to it, we tend to turn off and not assimilate this information. It is important to have the opportunity to look at it again when one is alone.

The leader might put sheets of paper on a table with a group member's name written on each sheet and invite the participants to write positive comments on each person's sheet. A fun way to do this is to invite everyone to tape a sheet of paper on another person's back. Give everyone markers and invite them to write positive comments on each person's back.

When everyone has finished writing the comments, each person reads the comments and takes a moment to assimilate them.

c) Invite the whole group to name how the Spirit was working with them today and call out the word or phrase into the centre as a form of closing prayer. End this prayer thanking the Spirit in whatever way is comfortable for you and your group.

MEDITATION

18

Balance

A Meditation on Achieving Balance in Life

Introduction

Preparation

- paper and pens for journalling
- copies of the questions asked in the meditation to give to the group before or after the meditation
- worship centre with candle, open Bible, bowl of water, rock, flowers or a plant, and images of balance, such as a balance toy
- CD player with appropriate background music
- bell to ring when shifting from writing to meditation
- hymn books to sing "Come and Find the Quiet Centre" (*Voices United* #374)

Read carefully the scriptures suggested.

Scripture

Luke: 12:22–32

Reflection

The passage from Luke invites us to live non-anxiously, in harmony with the flow of life, resting in and trusting in God. Verse 32 challenges us to live as though we believed that it is "God's good pleasure to give us the kingdom." Trusting in the benevolence of the universe is a spiritual challenge for most of us. Albert Einstein suggested that the key question is: "Is the universe friendly?"

I find when I can live out of gratitude for God's benevolence, in harmony with the flow of God's life through me, I am most at peace and filled with a sense of deep wholeness. However, balance is and continues to be a constant struggle in my own life. I seem to have spent much of my life alternating between overcommitment, with not enough space for self-care and play, and, in my longing for balance, moving into a state of almost lethargy with not enough stimulation or involvement.

In neither state do I find the peace and wholeness that comes from living in harmony with my body, mind, and spirit. The highs of committed involvement were and are wonderful. They can become addictive. Increasingly, I am aware of the price I pay when I do not attend to balance.

With experience, I find myself moving more into a state of balance, not stuck in the middle, but always moving back and forth over a centre point, always correcting for errors, but not too much and not too little.

Balance is a learned skill. It improves with practice, as with riding a bicycle, learning to skate, or learning tai chi. As we learn, we make mistakes and try again. Our hands, feet, and mind seem to be totally out of coordination. Something that looks so easy when an expert does it becomes much more complex when we try to put together the same combination of physical, mental, and spiritual practices. Sometimes out of fear or self-consciousness, we get totally lost.

It is hard to learn a new way of doing things, a new way of moving the body. It is tempting to give up and say I can never learn all those moves. It is hard to learn a new way of living in balance if this is not what we are used to. We are afraid to change patterns that have become so familiar. It feels strange to live from a different place, and it is easy to give up and go back to what feels familiar.

If we persevere, something happens in our body and mind. In my tai chi class, the moves that were impossible last week suddenly work this week. We find ourselves moving in a new way. We are flowing. Our feet move without conscious guidance. Head, arms, and hips move in a dynamic, coordinated alignment that happens effortlessly. What seemed nearly impossible a few moments earlier is happening, and we don't really know how we are doing it.

Living a balanced life is like this. At first, we struggle and find ourselves caught in the extremes. We eat too much or too little. We work too little, then we work too hard. We sleep too much or too little. We do this too much. We do that too little.

If we keep trying to balance our life, it gets easier. After many movements back toward the centre, eventually, some of our extreme behaviours lose their charm. We learn to sense when we are out of balance and we put it right. We have learned the point at which a little more will be too much, a little less will not be enough.

When we find this flowing balance, what we are doing becomes easy. Straining just interrupts the flow.

Gathering

a) Sing "Come and Find the Quiet Centre" (*Voices United* #374).

b) Share the Reflection or the parts that feel appropriate. Invite further reflection and ask for reactions.

c) Give copies of the questions to group members, asking them not to look at them until they are ready to journal.

Meditation

The second part of this meditation could include journalling or be carried out in silence. If you decide to use the journalling option, invite people to have the journals on their laps ready to begin at the appropriate time.

Sit quietly in an upright position ... Close your eyes ... Become aware of this body-self that is you, as you come to meditation today ... Focus on your breath ... Notice the pattern of your breathing ... as it moves in ... as it moves out ... Notice how fast you are breathing ... Notice whether you are breathing deeply or with shallow breaths ... Notice where your body moves when you breathe ... Is the movement in your chest ... or in your belly? ...

Watch your breathing for a few minutes and notice any changes that occur ... You may find that just attending to your breath will allow you to relax ... As you focus and breathe ... let your breaths become slower ... and deeper ... Let your body relax ... and move to a sense of peace ...

Notice where your body is sore or tense ... Imagine the breath moving to that place and gently massaging the tightened knots of tension ... or fear ... or anger ... Simply allow the breath to open up your body ... so that your life energy can flow freely ... You are preparing yourself for prayer ...

As you focus on your breathing ... you may notice thoughts coming and going ... Just notice the thoughts ... then let them go ... You may want to imagine them as clouds floating across the horizon ... or as leaves on a stream being carried away ... Just as your lungs generate breath ... your mind generates thoughts ... As thoughts arise ... gently return your focus to your breath ... Notice the space that opens inside you as you relax ... as you gradually come into your sacred centre ...

Ask God to bless this meditation journey ... and to use it for your highest good of mind ... body ... and spirit ...

Consider the lilies of the field ... Imagine that you are in a garden watching flowers and grasses bending in a gentle breeze ... Notice how the flowers move first in one direction ... gently flowing with the breeze ... then how they come back to the centre ... Another breeze comes from a slightly different direction, and the flowers bend with that breeze, swaying with the flow of the air ... But always they return to a balanced centre point ...

Imagine yourself as one of these flowers ... Imagine yourself moving in one direction ... then another ... to the back ... then to front ... Each time you come back to a place of perfect balance ... become acquainted with the sensation of perfect balance ...

Notice your breathing ... in breaths ... out breaths ... Not clinging to breathing in ... or out ... but flowing from one to the other ... As you relax and observe your breathing ... you may notice that the pause between inhaling and exhaling grows somewhat longer ... This is a balance point ... This is where your breathing is at equilibrium ... Don't cling to that balance point ... but be aware of it ... and let the inflow and outflow of air in your body meet there in harmony ... Let God's Spirit breathe you ...

As you rest in this sacred breath ... rest in God who desires to give you all that you need ... the kingdom ... Feel the balance that comes as you allow God's life to flow through you in trust ... Ask God to continue to teach you balance in your life ... Ask God to continue to teach you to trust life ... Ask God to continue to teach you to rest in the Spirit ...

(YOU MAY WISH TO OFFER TIME TO JOURNAL THE FOLLOWING QUESTIONS NOW OR TO REFLECT ON THEM IN MEDITATIVE SILENCE AND HAVE TIME TO JOURNAL AT THE END.)

Spend a few moments examining your lifestyle:

- Where is the balance? ...
- When do you feel life is flowing gracefully? ...
- Where in your life have you not yet learned balance? ...
- When do you feel you are struggling to stay upright? ... or to move ahead? ...
- What could you do to shift those unbalanced areas toward the centre? ...
- What behaviour could you do a little less of? ...
- What could you do a little more of? ...
- What do you fear about changing? ...
- What is your goal? ...

Take some time to see your goal of balanced life clearly ahead of you.

Imagine what your life would look like if your goal became a reality....

Breathing in ... feel yourself attaining perfect balance ...

Breathing out ... let go of your fear of change ...

Breathing in ... feel yourself attaining perfect balance ...

Breathing out ... let go of your fear of change ...

Breathing in ... feel yourself attaining perfect balance ...

Breathing out ... let go of your fear of change ...

(LONG PERIOD OF SILENCE)

As you are ready ... gradually connect with your body-self ... bringing with you the sense of harmony and balance with which you have connected ... Bring with you the goal of balance ... As you are ready ... open your eyes.

Silence

Allow the group time to work on the questions that they asked in the meditation. This time of journalling may be extended due to the nature of the questions asked.

Ring the bell at the end of the silent time to call people into the group again.

Debriefing

I would be inclined to debrief in small groups of two or three since there may be detailed and very personal sharing.

Closure

Invite participants to formulate some concrete intentions for working on balance in their lives, to write these down, and to share them with at least one other person in the group. (During the next session invite participants to share how they have been doing with their intentions. Do this for several weeks if this is an ongoing group.)

Close with prayer.

MEDITATION

19

Embracing Transformation

Introduction

This meditation reflects on the archetypal experience of letting go in order to experience new life. It is particularly useful for those who wish to move beyond what is blocking them from experiencing freedom.

Preparation

- paper and pens for journalling
- worship centre with cloth, candle, open Bible, a cross, symbols of transformation (a cocoon, photo of a butterfly, crystal, seed and plant), large stones
- CD player with background music
- bell to ring when shifting from writing to meditation

Reflect on your own experiences of transformation.

Scripture

John 11:1–44, John 12:24

Reflection

The death and resurrection story of Jesus speaks of transformation and letting go in order for life to multiply. Just when it seemed that everything was lost, when failure and death had the final word, resistant life burst free.

One does not have to take the physical resurrection of Jesus in a literal way to know the deep truth it embodies. Many of us have experienced being at the end of our rope, feeling as if it were "game over," when unexpectedly life finds a crack in the panic and fear, to bloom hope and possibility. A friend calls when we feel completely alone. There is a glimmer of reconciliation in a painful relationship. We find courage where we thought fear ruled our lives. We come home to ourselves when we thought we were lost. There are many "faces" of resurrection, of transformation. The life-death-life dynamic is there in them all.

As this meditation invites us into a cave, it would not be suitable for people who suffer severe claustrophobia or who have experienced involuntary confinement. Some may feel comfortable doing the meditation with "soft eyes," eyes that are half opened but not looking out to take in the exterior world.

In the middle of this meditation, people may choose to journal. If you use this option, ask people to have their journals and pens on their laps, ready to open part way through the meditation, while still staying in sacred inner space.

Gathering (Choose a or b)

a) Invite participants to share an experience that has felt transformative for them.
   - What are some of the qualities or characteristics of that experience?
   - Did you have any sense of God's presence in that experience?
   - What was that like?

b) Have you ever been inside a cave? Share that experience.

Meditation

Close your eyes ... Become aware of this body-self that is you, as you come to meditation today ... Focus on your breath ... Notice the pattern of your breathing ... as it moves in ... as it moves out ... Follow your breath in ... Follow your breath out ... Notice how fast you are breathing ... Notice whether you are breathing deeply or with shallow breaths ... Notice where your body moves when you breathe ... Is the movement in your chest ... or in your belly? ...

Watch your breathing for a few minutes ... notice any changes that occur ... You may find that just attending to your breath will allow you to relax ... As you focus and breathe, let your breaths become slower and deeper ... Let your body relax and move to a place of peace ...

Notice where your body is sore or tense ... Imagine the breath moving to that place ... and gently massaging the tightened knots of tension ... or fear ... or anger ... or stress ... Simply allow the breath to open up your body ... so that your life energy can flow freely ... You are preparing yourself for prayer.

As you focus on your breathing ... you may notice thoughts coming and going ... Just notice the thoughts ... then let them go ... You may want to imagine them as clouds floating across the horizon ... or as leaves on a stream being carried away ... As thoughts arise ... gently return your focus to your breath ... Notice the space that opens inside you as you relax ... as you gradually come into your sacred centre ...

Ask God to bless this meditation journey and to use it for your highest good of mind ... body ... and spirit ...

In your mind's eye ... see yourself going down a path ... You come to a dark wood ... This is a safe place ... where you are invited and protected by the Spirit ... You see someone ... a wisdom figure ... a Holy One, sent to take you deeper on your spiritual path ... This spiritual one embraces you as a long lost child ... looks lovingly into your eyes ... offers to be your guide ... If you allow it, the Holy One takes your hand ... You go deep into the forest together ... This is a safe place ... and you are with the One who desires your highest good ...

You come to a cave cut out of a rock ... Enter the cave with your guide ... Feel the walls ... the floor ... listen for the sounds in the cave ... Know that this is a place for your spiritual transformation ... a place for you to let go ... and to release things that keep you from fullness of life ... Your guide places a stone across the entrance ...

This Holy One asks you to reflect on stones that are blocks in your own life ...

What are those stony walls that stifle your living ... the stones that keep you walled in the stony, silent place of un-living? ...

What are the stones that block your way to communion with God ... that block your creativity ... that block your livingness ... your being fully alive to be all that God intends you to be? ...

What is the stone that blocks the way to the light and the freedom of life in all its fullness? ...

What is the stone that blocks out fresh air ... that keeps you just breathing and recycling the same old stuff over and over again? ...

What is the stone that keeps you from accessing the sacred right that is yours as a child of God? ...

The stone may be fear that keeps you paralyzed ... or makes you run away ... fear that binds you ...

The stone may be powerlessness ... that immobilizes you from taking on your life ... that keeps you cut off from your sacred source ... locked in the victim role ...

The stone may be alienation that keeps you lonely ... neglected and neglecting ... It keeps you from belonging ... and from inviting others to belong ...

The stone may be addiction ... to substance ... to work ... to perfection ... to things ...

The stone may be anger and hurt held on to for far too long ...

Whatever your stone is ... allow the Spirit who is with you to help you name it ...

(AT THIS POINT, YOU MAY INVITE PEOPLE TO WRITE IN THEIR JOURNALS FOR A WHILE BEFORE RESUMING THE MEDITATION. CONTINUE WHEN IT SEEMS THAT PEOPLE HAVE FINISHED WITH THEIR WRITING. YOU MAY RING A BELL TO SIGNAL THE CHANGE FROM WRITING TO MEDITATING.)

Then hear the Spirit ... call you to come to life ... to come out from the tomb ... as Jesus invited Lazarus before his own death ...

"Come to life ... Come out ... You do not need to stay in this stifling place ... You can let go of this stone that confines you ... Be free ..."

And the stone, which you could not move by yourself, begins to move ... Notice the stone as it begins to shake and allow the first glimmers of light into the cave ... Smell the first breath of fresh air as it comes into the cave ... As you get a taste for new life ... hunger for more freedom ... more light ... more space ... Hunger to be released from this confining place ... And let this hunger strengthen you ... so that the stone keeps moving and rolling away ... creating more and more space ... and more and more light ... and more and more fresh air ... and more and more new life in you ...

As you are ready, step out into the freedom of new life ... What does it feel like to step out into the fresh air? ... What do you first notice? ... Let yourself drink in the experience of freedom ... and of new life ...

Your Wise Guide gives you a treasure box ... It is not very large ... and you feel for the lid ... It is filled with radiant, loving light ... The light comes slowly out of the box ... and surrounds you ... and fills you ... permeates your whole being ... It is holy light ... Receive this light ... enjoy it ... Let it fill the spaces left by letting go ...

As you leave ... you carry the box ... knowing the light is with you ... and that freedom and abundant new life are yours ...

When you feel ready ... gradually draw yourself back to this place ... Notice your breath ... notice your body-self as it is sitting in the chair ... Feel the bottom of your feet as they connect you with the earth ... Gradually make some gentle movements with your toes and fingers ... some circles with your shoulders and head ... When you are ready open your eyes ...

Silence

Provide a time for those who wish to journal.

Ring the bell at the end of the silent time to call people into the group again.

Debriefing

- How was God with you in your meditation today?
- What did you experience?

Closure

From the experience of the meditation, write down some aspect of new life that you intend to claim. Name it to the others in the group. Take it home and put it in a visible place to remind you of your intention to claim new, transformed life.

MEDITATION

20

Where Is Your Treasure?

Introduction

Preparation

- paper and pens for journalling
- CD player with appropriate background music
- bell to ring when shifting from writing to meditation
- worship centre with cloth, candle, bowl of water, stone, box with lid in which to place things that you treasure

If it is an ongoing group, you could ask people to bring to this session something that they treasure and can share. They can place these treasures in the worship centre.

Scripture

Luke 12:32–34

Reflection

In scripture, the heart is used as a metaphor for the core self. Marcus Borg, in his book *The Heart of Christianity*[17], has a wonderful chapter on the opening of the heart. He discusses the biblical understanding of the heart as the image of the self at a deep level, as the spiritual centre of the total self. When our hearts are open, Borg says, we are able to see more clearly with eyes opened by Spirit. We are able to understand more deeply because our hearts are opened to sense beyond the surface. When our hearts are open, we are more connected with gratitude, with compassion, with wonder and awe. When our hearts are open, we remember God and know that we are created to walk in God's way of justice. Where our heart is will determine where our life's centre will be, where our life's energies will be directed, where our resources of time and money will be invested.

In today's scripture, Jesus invites us to notice what we treasure and then we will know where our heart truly is. This meditation allows us to reflect on what we are doing with our lives, how we are spending our time, our energy, our money, so that we might know where our heart is, and whether our heart is where we desire it to be.

In an era deeply concerned with "affluenza," and unjust distribution of wealth and power, it is important for people of faith to reflect on the relationship of our heart and our treasure. I hope this meditation will be helpful for individuals and groups that want to pursue that kind of spiritual assessment so that they can bring their lives more into line with their core values.

Gathering (Choose a, b, or c)

a) Get in touch with something that you really treasure and share this with the group (or see the suggestion in Preparation above).

b) Imagine yourself at the age of five as clearly as you are able. What did you treasure then? at 18? What do you treasure now? Share how what you treasure has changed or remained the same. You can do this as a written exercise for sharing.

c) Read Luke 12:32–34. Reflect on your insights.

Meditation

You can use this meditation in a variety of ways. One might lead the meditation as far as "Let it fill your whole being," then the rest could be done as journalling in response to the questions. One could also stay in meditation state and have space for writing or reflecting, then invite journalling at the end.

Close your eyes ... Let yourself pay attention to what it feels like to be in this body-self that is you right now ... Most of us go through whole days, sometimes our whole lives, without really paying attention to this body-self.... In Hebrew (the language system Jesus knew), there was no such thing as disembodied spirit ... They spoke of the *nephesh* ... the body soul ... the spirit body.... Jesus talked about our bodies as temples of the Spirit ... What is it like for you to think of yourself in that way? ...

As you begin to pay attention to your body, do you notice places where tension is stored up ... where your muscles are in tight knots? ... As you scan your body, from the top of your head to the bottom of your feet ... notice if there are tender places or sore spots ... Send compassion to these places in your body, thanking them for the hard work they are doing ... perhaps offering to pay more attention to what they are telling you in the future ...

Become aware of your breathing ... Our breath connects us with all that has been here since the beginning of creation ... Breathing ... this life-giving process that goes on all of the time, even when we are unaware ... Notice if you are breathing with only a small part of your lungs ... or whether you are taking the breath deeply into your whole being ... down to the bottom of your lungs ... up to the tops of your shoulders ... Notice if your tummy moves in and out as you inhale and as you exhale ... the way a baby's does when it is breathing naturally ... before its body has become tensed and locked up with the stress of living ...

Most of us breathe using only a small part of our lung capacity ... in bodies tightened up ... not fully open to the breath of life ... Let your body relax ... Let the tension flow out of your body through your feet ... Begin to allow your breath to move deeper into your being ... taking the breath deep down into your belly ... creating inner space ...

Breathe in deeply the healing presence of God ... the goodness and grace of God ... Take it right into the core of your being ... As you breathe out ... let the breath carry with it the poisons ... physical ... emotional ... and spiritual that have built up in your system ...

Breathe in the newness of possibility ... the hope that God gives ... Let go of the stress and tensions that are stored in your body-self ... in your emotional self ... in your spiritual self ...

Breathe in life energy ... the creating breath of God that was there from the beginning ... Breathe out whatever would block you from being fully present to this time ...

Again notice your body ... If there continue to be tense places, imagine this healing breath moving directly to those spots ... loosening the tension ... letting go ...

letting be ... letting open ... letting unlock ... Notice the inner space that is being prepared and opened up inside you ... space for the sacred presence to find room ... space for the Holy One to be with you ... your own sacred space ... your own holy ground.

In that sacred place ... I invite you to reflect on your own treasure ... Imagine yourself beside a beautiful river on a warm summer afternoon ... The waves are lapping ... the breeze gently moves the leaves in the trees ... Know that you are part of this sacred creation ... Let yourself relax into the presence of the God who created all of this ...

Imagine Jesus coming to be with you in this place ... in this sacred spot ... Imagine Jesus looking deeply into your eyes ... clear through to the centre of your soul ... and telling you that you do not need to be afraid ... that God's heart's desire is to give you the kingdom ... God's delight would be to give you life in all its fullness ... shalom ... God longs to be with you in such a way that you do not need to be afraid ... so that you might know that you are not alone ... Notice how you feel about this promise ...

Let this promise be in your heart ... Feel the light and the power of God's desire for you in your heart ... Let that light grow and strengthen ... Let it fill your whole being ...

Then in the presence of this promise ... let Jesus invite you to look with him at your life and your priorities ... what do you really treasure? ...

Where is your heart? ...

In what do you invest and spend your life force? ...

Where do you put your energy? ...

Where do you spend your time? ...

For what or for whom would you give your life? ...

Remembering God's desire to give you life in all its fullness ... take a long, loving look at your life and your priorities:

- What insights does God offer you? ...
- What can you do more of in your life? ...
- What can you do less? ...

(LONG SPACE FOR REFLECTION AND OPPORTUNITY TO JOURNAL)

If you were to imagine yourself at the point of your death ... as you look back over your life ... what would have been most important? ... What would you call your treasure? ... What would have been really valuable and lasting? ... Where does your relationship with God fit in? ... Spend some time with Christ reflecting on these questions ...

How do you feel about what is coming up for you? ...

What do you want to do about it? ...

(LONG SPACE FOR REFLECTION AND OPPORTUNITY TO JOURNAL)

As you are ready ... take some time of gratitude for the treasure that is yours ... for the place where your heart is ...

Again, connect with the fullness in your heart as you remember God's love for you ... and God's desire to give you the kingdom ... God's delight to give you life in all its fullness ...

Gradually and gently draw yourself back into this body-self that is you today ... Notice the breath again ... Take some deep breaths as you reconnect with your body ... Make some gentle movements with your toes, your fingers, your head ... and when you are ready, open your eyes.

Silence

Allow the meditation to set in the conscious mind and continue any journalling participants might desire to do.

Ring the bell at the end of the silent time to call people into the group again.

Debriefing

a) Share what happened for you.
   - How was God for you in this time of meditative prayer?
   - What happened when you allowed Christ to sit with you as you looked at your priorities?

b) If you chose the option of silent reflection on the questions in the body of the meditation, then give each person in the group a copy of the questions on which space has been left between the questions for a written response.

Invite them to note any insights they received from the Sacred Source during the meditation about changes that they need to make, or areas that need more attention, and areas that God invites them to develop.

Home Soul Work

a) Write the changes desired as intentions. This means putting the challenge in a positive form, imagining that you are achieving them, for example: "I am taking personal quiet time and space because I am worth it and I need this time with God and with myself." "I choose wisely how I will spend my time, my energy, my life for my own health and wholeness."

b) Put these in a convenient place, such as on the refrigerator door or your computer, to remind you regularly of your desire for these intentions that God invites you to develop.

c) Pray these intentions (simply focus on the intention and invite God's Spirit to surround it) for the next week and notice what happens as you do this, for example:

If, through the meditation, people recognized that they were not paying enough attention to a particular relationship, their creative self, their justice-making self, their self-care, or their relationship with God, an intention might be "to grow in paying attention and making space and time for these things." Each day the person would remember the intention in God's presence and give it prayer energy and imagine himself or herself living according to this intention.

Closure

Share something that happened for you in this experience that opened your heart. The leader can close with a prayer that expresses gratitude for these movements of Spirit.

Part VI

Meditations for Pastoral Care

MEDITATION

21

A Touch of Compassion

Introduction

This is a meditation for those who wish to deepen their compassion for those who suffer. It will be of particular interest to those who offer pastoral care or for those who plan pastoral care training.

Preparation

The meditation is written for those meditating at the bedside of someone who is suffering. However, you could lead it with a pastoral care team and invite them to follow it in their imagination and to discuss afterwards.

For a Group

- worship centre with symbols of compassion, such as a heart, cross, pictures of people in need of compassion or offering compassion
- pencils and papers for journalling
- CD player with appropriate music

Scripture

Matthew 5:3–10 (or scripture that focuses on compassion, such as v. 3, 4, 5, 7, 8), Matthew 14:14, Matthew 15:32, Matthew 20:34, Mark 1:41, Luke 7:13, Luke 10:33, Luke 15:20

Use any of the stories that show Jesus' compassion, for example, his reaching out to touch lepers, healing Jairus' daughter, healing the blind man, or the story of the man with the withered arm (see above scriptures).

Reflection

"To train in compassion, then, is to know all beings are the same and suffer in similar ways, to honour all those who suffer, and to know you are neither separate from nor superior to anyone."[18]

"When he went ashore, he saw a large crowd; and he had compassion for them and cured their sick." Matthew 14:14

When Jesus speaks of having "compassion," he would be using the Hebrew word *rechem*. This word is related to the Hebrew word for womb. Compassion has a connection with the powerful experience of womb-love, the kind of love a mother who has given birth feels for her child. This word is often used in Hebrew scripture for God's love for us.[19]

In scripture, whenever there is compassion, a person or God changes heart and is also moved to act with loving kindness and healing toward another. Sometimes it is to feed, sometimes to heal, sometimes to intervene with justice, sometimes to reconcile, sometimes to care. But compassion and a loving response to a situation or person always go side by side in scripture.

The challenge is how to put into practice the compassion we feel, especially when we are face to face with suffering. Many of us struggle with what we can do when someone is suffering. What is our response when we know someone is dying?

Sometimes we avoid being with those who suffer by getting involved in other things. Somehow, we just never get around to that visit. It is easier to stay caught up in busy lives than to reach out to a person in pain, to visit the sick person, to be with a person who is dying.

What makes us do this? Fear perhaps. Maybe we are afraid that we won't know what to say or are afraid that the other may see how uncomfortable we are. Maybe we are afraid to see the pain of the other because it reminds us of our own mortality or of the pain we may have to confront in similar circumstances.

Giving in to these fears leads us to avoidance and guilt. Overcoming these fears may lead to an experience of love, compassion, and an opportunity to ease another's pain. It can help us face our own suffering so that we will not have to avoid another's pain.

Here is a meditation that may help you to be with a sick person in a way that may be useful for both of you. You can follow this meditation in your imagination, thinking of the person you want to visit, or you can meditate in the room with the person in silent space. You can also use this meditation with a pastoral care team to help open up their heart of compassion for those who suffer.

Meditation

Use this meditation if you are with the person.

If you are meditating in the room with the person who is ill, first of all sit with her or him for a while and talk with her or him. If she or he is conscious and if it feels appropriate, say, "May I just sit quietly with you for a while? Let's just be in God's presence together for a while in silence." If it seems appropriate, you might take the person's hand in yours. If you do not know the person well, you may ask, "Do you mind if I hold your hand?" If you put your hand under the person's hand, he or she can always withdraw it whenever he or she wishes.

Still yourself as you prepare to be with the person who is ill ... Notice your breath as it moves in ... as it moves out ... Let each breath move more deeply into your body ... Notice your tummy as it rises with the breath in ... as it falls with the breath out ... Continue to pay attention to the breath as you bring yourself into a place of peace and stillness ...

Look into the person's eyes, if the eyes are open ... Look at the person's face ... What emotions do you see there? ... What experience is written on the person's face? ... Look at that face and imagine the story and the wonder of a life lived ... Notice the compassion that arises in you as you look lovingly at the face of this person who is ill ...

Gently hold the hand in yours ... Feel the life energy there ... Notice if the hand is warm or cool ... Be aware of the person's hand in your hand ... Imagine God's Spirit of healing and compassion opening up a new channel of compassion and love between you ... Imagine the energy of compassion flowing through you to the person through your hands ...

Notice what is happening in your heart ... What feelings are you having? ... Look for the seed of compassion ... Let it grow ... Let your heart open until it is filled with loving compassion ... with warmth ... with the light of God's Spirit of love and compassion ... Let this light grow in your heart ... Let it grow so that it fills your whole body ... and fills the entire room ... Remind yourself that love and compassion are limitless and that they fill the universe ...

Imagine that the love of God is a light that shines on you and upon the person you are sitting with ... Let that love shower you with light and empower your spirit ... Imagine your mind, body, and spirit opening to all the love and compassion in the world and allow that love and compassion to flow through you into this other person ... See the light shining in your heart flowing through you to the other ...

Feel the compassion of God flowing through you to him or her... The supply is limitless so you will not feel depleted ... Feel your life energy grow as you draw it in from the world ... Feel it passing to your companion ...

Silently say to yourself, "May you rest in the light of God's healing love ... may you be free of suffering ... may Christ's heart of compassion hold you...." Extend this wish to yourself and to the other person ...

Sit this way for several minutes ... While you are passing loving energy to your companion, remain aware of her or his subtle responses to you ... Avoid becoming lost in your own process ... You are there for your companion ... You are responsive to her or his needs ... You are sensitive to her or his fatigue and the passage of time ... You know when to withdraw and take care to leave before your presence becomes a burden ... Yet you are willing to stay with your companion in God's light of compassion as long as this seems helpful ... Before you withdraw ... offer a blessing to the person: "May you rest in the light of God's healing love...." After you have withdrawn ... again shower yourself with the light of God's compassionate love ... Bathe your whole being ... mind ... body ... and spirit in the compassionate loving-kindness of God ... Offer yourself a blessing as you say to yourself, "May I rest in the light of God's healing love."

MEDITATION

22

Meditation for Those Facing Surgery

Reflection

As a minister, I often sit with people who are heading into surgery and know the fear and anxiety that builds up as the uncertainty of what lies ahead escalates. I have been told that when people undergo anaesthesia, they wake up in the same emotional state in which they entered sleep. In approaching my own surgeries, I decided that I surely did not want to awaken on the other side of surgery with fear and anxiety as well as pain.

So I used this meditation myself just before surgery as I was waiting outside the operating room. Since then I have suggested it to many others who have found it useful. On several occasions, I have been present, as their minister, to lead them through it.

Meditation

Relax and allow yourself to be in touch with the breath of life that moves in and out of your body ... As you breathe, take the breath deep into your body ... As you breathe ... take in the goodness and grace of God ... And let the breath out carry with it any fear that you can release ... Breathe in God's desire for wholeness for you ... and breathe out anxiety that has built up in your body ... Imagine it flowing out of every cell of your body as you breathe out ... With each breath in ... take in God's healing presence ... With each breath out let yourself relax into the hands of God who works through the hands of the surgeons and nurses ...

Fill your body with light as you breathe in the breath of God ... Fill your heart with healing light ... Let it still your feelings and bring you deep peace ... Fill your mind with healing light ... Let it still your thoughts as you focus on your healing ... Fill your whole body with healing light so that your body is open to the flow of God's healing love and energy ... Fill the particular area of your body where you are having surgery with healing light ... Surround your body with healing, protective light ... so that Spirit is present to you as you enter surgery ...

Ask that God be present in the hands and minds and hearts of those who operate on you so that all might be for the highest good of mind, body, and spirit ... Invite the risen, healer Christ to be in the room as your surgery proceeds ... guiding those who will operate on you ...

Gather the love and the prayers of family and friends who care for you ... Gather that strength and healing energy into your body ... into your mind ... into your spirit ...

Continue to imagine yourself filled and surrounded with light ... accompanied by the risen, healer Christ ... and the blessing and guidance of the Holy Spirit ... the love and healing prayer of friends and family as you enter surgery ...

MEDITATION

23

Communal Preparation of a Patient for Surgery

If a person is part of a spiritual community or surrounded by a supportive community or family, invite the person to sit on a chair and have friends and family gather in a healing, blessing circle around him or her. You might use the meditation The Tree of Life (see page 43) as preparation, or you might choose to do the following:

Lay hands on the person (if touch is comfortable for the person) or hold hands out in blessing (if this is more comfortable).

Invite each person to image the healing light of God's love, the heart of Christ's compassion flowing through his or her hands as a blessing on the person who is ill.

Ask that the healing power of God flow into the person's mind, body, and spirit.

Ask that the strength of God's healing presence flow into the person's mind, body, and spirit.

Ask that the compassion of Christ's heart of love flow into the person's mind, body, and spirit.

Ask that the presence of God's Spirit guide those who care for the person who is ill.

You may offer vocal prayer or pray in silence. You may invite individuals to offer words of blessing to the person who is ill.

Sometimes a concrete symbol of the gathered blessings of the community is very helpful. This could be a stone or shell into which the blessings and prayers of those gathered have been symbolically placed. There may be another symbol that speaks to the specific person or need such as a stuffed toy for a child.

Tell the person that you will all be holding him or her in the healing light of God as he or she undergoes surgery and make sure that you do this at the time of surgery. In my congregation, some have chosen to light a candle when they know one of our circle is having surgery, offering it as a continuous prayer for the other.

MEDITATION

24

Meditation for Those Undergoing Chemotherapy Treatment

Reflection

It was only after people told me that they used some of the tracks of the CD *The Healing Oasis* during their chemotherapy treatments that I thought of developing a meditation particularly for this use.

It can be a long and often stressful process to receive certain types of chemotherapy. It is hard for the body to embrace something that functions as a poison even though it may be the best option. Dr. Bernie Siegal has found that the openness of the patient makes a great difference to the effectiveness of various treatments. Dr. Siegal suggests that those who emotionally and spiritually reject and fear a treatment will not find their treatment as effective as do those who are able to embrace it for their healing.[20]

This meditation is not meant to replace medical treatment, but to accompany it and strengthen its effectiveness. It is dangerous to suggest that meditation is a magical cure.

There is a difference between healing and curing. Yet there are many stories of people whose cancer has disappeared as their lives were being healed. There are others whose cancer does not disappear, yet they die as healed people in a place of peace and acceptance.

Increasingly, we are coming to know the connection of mind, body, and spirit. To me, it only makes sense that we use the power of the mind and spirit in our fight for health and life. If we are able to imagine the taste of a lemon and notice how it affects our saliva flow, if we are able to slow our heart beat by practising meditation and relaxation, then surely it is not far-fetched to suggest that using healing imagery may also have an effect on the body.

There is much literature that can explain research on the power of prayer much better than I can. If you are living with cancer or other life-threatening illness, I encourage you to read these books. Larry Dossey,[21] a medical doctor, suggests that in the future, if doctors do not pray with their patients, it will be considered malpractice, because they have not used all the tools that they have at their disposal for healing and health.

I offer this simple meditation as part of one's toolkit to support healing.

Meditation

Be in touch with your breath as you notice it moving in and out of your body ... You may find that the tension of being where you are has tightened your body ... There may be knots of tension in your shoulders ... in your stomach ... in your head ... As you breathe, let your body relax and let go ...

Breathe in the breath of life ... Let it move deep into your body ... mind ... and spirit ... Breathe out fear and anxiety and release them as you are able to do so ...

Breathe in life ... breathe out fear and anxiety ...

Breathe in life ... breathe out fear and anxiety ...

Breathe in the grace of God ... letting it gently take root in your body ...

Breathe out the tension and stress in the cells of your body ...

Breathe in God's grace ... breathe out tension and stress ...

Breathe in God's grace ... breathe out tension and stress ...

Breathe in the healing strength of God ... Breathe out whatever blocks you from being fully present ...

Breathe in healing strength ... breathe out what blocks you ...

Breathe in healing strength ... breathe out what blocks you ...

Let the breath gradually still your soul ... Let the breath gradually still your spirit ... Let the breath gradually still your mind ... Let the breath gradually still your body ...

As you notice your body-self right now ... notice where you are storing tension ... fear ... anger ... Ask those parts of your body if there is any message they want you to hear ...

Imagine the breath moving directly to those places ... gently and lovingly massaging ... loosening the tension ... Feel the muscles relax and let go as you offer them this healing ... loving care and attention ...

Keep doing this until your body is deeply relaxed ... opened to the flow of the Spirit and energy ...

Be in touch with your need for healing ... Allow the desire for healing to grow more and more strongly within you ... Thank your body for the work it is doing to restore you to health ...

Fill your body with compassion for the struggle it is going through ...

Fill your body with love and unconditional acceptance ...

Fill your body with knowing that you are more than your disease ...

Fill your body with knowing that you are a deeply beloved child of God ... Allow that love ... and the experience of that love ... to flow in your mind ... in your spirit ... in your body ... And notice what happens to your body as you allow it to be filled with this compassion ... with this unconditional love ... with this loving acceptance ...

Invite each cell of your body to restore itself to the wholeness and health that was God's original intention for it ... Imagine the chemotherapy you are receiving moving into your body, working to restore your cells to health and wholeness ... Feel it flow into your being with an intention for healing ... Imagine it going into the place where your cancer is ... Imagine it working to shrink and to eradicate any unhealthy cells ... Imagine the cells in the affected area being transformed into healthy cells ... building health for your body ... There may be a particular image that has power for you as you image this healing taking place ... You may wish to image a tumour shrinking and gradually disappearing ... You may have other images that are healing for you ... Notice any image the Spirit would give you ...

In your mind's eye ... see the chemotherapy working to cleanse ... to heal ... to free your body of any cancer cells ...

In your mind's eye, see the affected area free from cancer ... filled with healthy cells and tissue ... Hold that image in your mind ... in your heart ... in your intention ... as you ask God's Spirit to keep bathing you with healing wholeness ...

Feel the healing, strengthening power of the Spirit as it fills your mind ... your body ... your spirit ...

Feel the Spirit bathing you with accepting, unconditional love ...

Feel the Spirit bathing every cell of your body with forgiveness ...

Feel the Spirit bathing every cell of your body with compassion ...

Feel the Spirit bathing you with healing for your mind ... with healing for your memories ... with healing for your life ... with healing for your feelings ... with healing for your body ...

Feel the Spirit bathe you with vitality ...

Feel the Spirit bathe you with energy that flows freely in you ...

Feel the Spirit bathing every cell of your body with hope ...

Rest in this flow of love and life as long as you need to and when you are ready, gradually draw yourself back to this place ... knowing that you bring the healing images planted in your mind, body, and spirit with you ... and that they will continue to work in you after this meditation is over ...

Endnotes

[1]Dr. Stephan Rechtschaffen, *Time Shifting* (New York: Broadway Books, 1997).

[2]Tara Bennett-Goleman, *Emotional Alchemy, How the Mind Can Heal the Heart* (New York: Harmony Books, 2001).

[3]John 3:8

[4]Claudio Naranjo, cited in David Fontana, *The Mediator's Handbook: Comprehensive Guide to Eastern and Western Mediation Techniques* (Rockport, MA: Element, 1992).

[5]Carolyn Stahl, *Opening to God: Guided Imagery Meditation on Scripture for Individuals and Groups* (Nashville: The Upper Room, 1977).

[6]One of the best dictionaries of symbols is: Ad de Vries, *Dictionary of Symbols and Imagery* (New York: North-Holland Publishing Co., 1984).

[7]Healing Pathway is a program of the Naramata Centre of The United Church of Canada, in British Columbia. It is part of the Pathway to Healing and Wholeness.

[8]Joan Chittester, *There Is a Season* (Mary Knoll, New York: Orbis Books, 1995).

[9]Glastonbury is a small town 125 miles west of London.

[10]Andy Park, *The River Is Here* (Anaheim, CA: Mercy/Vineyard Publishing, 1997).

[11]Joan Chittester, *There Is a Season* (Mary Knoll, New York: Orbis books, 1995), p. 3.

[12]"Abba Father," *Glory and Praise*, Second Edition (Portland, Oregon: Oregon Catholic Press, 1997). It is sung by Rev. Carey Landry.

[13]"Earthen Vessels," *Glory and Praise*, Second Edition (Portland, Oregon: Oregon Catholic Press, 1997). It is sung by the St. Louis Jesuits.

[14]"A New Creed," *Voices United: The Hymn and Worship Book of The United Church of Canada* (The United Church Publishing House, 2003, reprint), p. 918.

[15]Some of this material was shared at Maritime Conference of The United Church of Canada in May 2005.

[16]*The New English Bible* © Oxford University Press and Cambridge University Press, 1961, 1970.

[17] Marcus Borg, *The Heart of Christianity: Rediscovering a Life of Faith* (HarperSanFrancisco, 2004), Chapter 8, "Thin Places; Opening the Heart," pp. 148-163.

[18]Sogyal Rinpoche, *The Tibetan Book of Living and Dying* (Toronto: Harper Collins Canada, 2004).

[19]See Rosemary Radford Ruether, *Sexism and God Talk, Toward a Feminist Theology* (Boston: Beacon Press, 1983), p. 56.

[20]Dr. Bernie Siegal, *Love, Medicine, and Modern Miracles* (New York: Harper and Row, 1986). See Bibliography for other books by Bernie Siegal.

[21]Larry Dossey, *Healing Words* (New York: Harper Collins, 1993). See Bibliography for other books by Larry Dossey.

[22] Flora Slosson Wuellner, *Prayer, Fear and our Powers* (Nashville: Upper Room, 1989). See Bibliography for other books by Flora Wuellner.

Bibliography

Bennett-Goleman, Tara, *Emotional Alchemy, How the Mind Can Heal the Heart* (New York: Harmony Books, 2001).

Borg, Marcus, *The Heart of Christianity: Rediscovering a Life of Faith* (HarperSanFrancisco, 2004).

Borysenko, Joan, *Minding the Body, Mending the Mind* (New York: Bantam Books, 1988).

Brueggemann, Walter, *Deep Memory and Exuberant Hope* (Augsberg: Fortress Canada, 2003).

––, *Hopeful Imagination; Prophetic Voices in Exile* (Augsberg: Fortress Canada, 2003).

––, *Introduction to the Old Testament: the Canon and Christian Imagination* (Louisville, London: Westminster John Knox Press, 2003).

––, *Prophetic Imagination* (Augsberg: Fortress Canada, 1978).

––, *Spirituality of the Psalms* (Augsberg: Fortress Canada, 2001).

Chittester, Joan,*There is a Season* (Mary Knoll, New York: Orbis Books, 1995).

Dossey, Dr. Larry, *Be Careful What You Pray For* (New York: Harper Collins, 1998).

––, *Healing Words,The Power of Prayer and the Practice of Medicine* (New York: Harper Collins, 1993).

––, *Prayer is Good Medicine* (New York: Harper Collins, 1996).

Eden, Donna, *Energy Medicine* (New York: Jeremy P. Tarcher/Putnam, 1999).

Graham, Rochelle, Flora Litt, and Wayne Irwin, *Healing from the Heart* (Kelowna B.C.: Wood Lake Books, 1998).

Park, Andy, *The River Is Here* (Anaheim, CA: Mercy/Vineyard Publishing, 1997).

Radford Ruether, Rosemary, *Sexism and God Talk, Toward a Feminist Theology* (Boston: Beacon Press, 1983).

Rechtschaffen, Stephan, *Time Shifting* (New York: Broadway Books, 1997).

Siegal, Dr. Bernie, *How to Live Between Office Visits: A Guide To Life, Love and Health* (New York: HarperCollins, 1993).

––, *Love, Medicine, and Modern Miracles* (New York: Harper and Row, 1986).

––, *Peace, Love, and Healing* (New York: Harper and Row, 1989).

Wuellner, Flora Slosson, *Heart of Healing, Heart of Light* (Nashville: Upper Room, 1992).

––, *Prayer and Our Bodies* (Nashville: Upper Room, 1987).

––, *Prayer, Fear and Our Powers* (Nashville: Upper Room, 1989).

––, *Release* (Nashville: Upper Room, 1996).

www.gracecathedral.org/labyrinth/.

Scripture Index

Also from Sharon Moon

The Healing Oasis
Guided Meditations for Mind, Body, and Spirit

It was the success of *The Healing Oasis* that prompted Sharon Moon to write its sequel. *The Healing Oasis* provides a moving series of guided meditations designed to connect us with the depths of our own experience in partnership with a loving, healing God. It includes helpful preparation and leadership suggestions for any circumstance, from congregational use to person reflection.

The Healing Oasis - CD

A CD of meditations, drawn from *The Healing Oasis*, is also available, individually or as a package.

$18.95 book
$9.95 CD
$25 book and CD package

Order today from UCRD, 1-800-288-7365 or 416-253-5456.